BERLITZ

Englisch
ÜBUNGSBUCH

Lynne Strugnell

© 1995 Berlitz Publishing Co., Ltd.

Handwriting font © Henry Bloomfield 1994

Berlitz Publishing Co., Ltd., Berlitz House, Peterley Road, Oxford OX4 2TX, UK

Berlitz Publishing Co., Inc., 257 Park Avenue South, New York, NY 10010, USA

Alle Rechte vorbehalten, insbesondere das Recht der Vervielfältigung und Verbreitung sowie der Übersetzung. Ohne schriftliche Genehmigung des Verlags ist es nicht gestattet, den Inhalt dieses Werks oder Teile daraus auf elektronischem oder mechanischem Wege (Fotokopie, Mikrofilm, Ton- und Bildaufzeichnung, Speicherung auf Datenträger oder ein anderes Verfahren) zu reproduzieren, zu vervielfältigen oder zu verbreiten.

Berlitz International, Inc., und ihre Tochtergesellschaften sind weltweit die einzigen Eigentümer des Namens Berlitz in bezug auf Sprachunterricht, Sprachlehrbücher, Sprachtonbänder und -kassetten sowie Sprachschulen. Der Gebrauch des Namens Berlitz ist anderen ausdrücklich untersagt, es sei denn, dies wurde von Berlitz durch formellen Vertrag erlaubt. Der Kauf oder Wiederverkauf dieses Titels oder irgendeiner anderen Veröffentlichung von Berlitz berechtigt weder den Käufer noch jede andere Person, den Namen Berlitz in Zusammenhang mit Sprachunterricht und in jeder anderen Verbindung zu gebrauchen.

Berlitz ist ein beim US Patent Office und in anderen Ländern eingetragenes Warenzeichen.

ISBN 0-7511-0867-7

1. Ausgabe—2. Auflage 1995

Printed in UK

INHALT

Einleitung 4

1: Alles über mich. Name; Adresse; Sichvorstellen; Nationalitäten. 5

2: Ich habe einen neuen Job. Familie; Alter; Beruf. 9

3: Wo ist Ihr Büro? Lage; Gebäude und ihre Einrichtungen; Farben. 13

4: Liebst du mich? Uhrzeit; Sport und Hobbys; was man mag und nicht mag. 17

5: Sind Sie morgen abend frei? Tägliche Aktivitäten; Häufigkeit; Uhrzeit; Wochentage. 21

6: Wieviel kostet das? Einkaufen; nach Artikeln fragen; Geld und Preise; Bekleidung; Größen. 25

7: Die Kneipe ist dort unten. Richtungen; Geschäfte und öffentliche Gebäude; Öffnungszeiten. 29

8: Wie war das Wochenende? Die Vergangenheit; Wochenendaktivitäten; *Wh*-Fragen 33

9: Wir sind zelten gefahren. Weitere Übungen zur Vergangenheit; Urlaub; Verkehrsmittel; Jahre. 37

10: Möchten Sie nun bestellen? Restaurants; Bestellen; Einkaufen; Maße und Gewichte. 41

11: Können Sie Französisch? Dinge, die man kann und die man nicht kann; Jobs; Gründe. 45

12: Wiederholung 49

13: Wie sieht sie aus? Wie man Leute beschreibt; Vergleich von Dingen; Körperteile. 53

14: Ich amüsier' mich ganz toll! Was gerade geschieht; Wetter; *so* bei Begründungen 57

15: Hast du morgen etwas vor? Die Zukunft; Pläne machen; Einladungen; Vorschläge; Daten. 61

16: Kommen Sie oft hierher? Smalltalk; Besitz; um Erlaubnis fragen und Erlaubnis erteilen; Häufigkeit. 65

17: Ich werde viel zu tun haben. Weitere Übungen zum Futur; Voraussagen; um Informationen bitten 69

18: Hin und zurück, bitte. Fahrkarten kaufen; Fahrpläne; höfliche Bitten. 73

19: Mir geht's schrecklich! Gesundheit und Sport; wie man sich fühlt; Ratschläge; Körperteile. 77

20: Er schläft noch. Über Erfahrungen sprechen; Dauer. 81

21: Na, wie geht's dir? Freunde treffen; was geschehen ist; wann etwas geschah. 85

22: Was für eine Katastrophe! Futur mit *will*; Wahrscheinlichkeit 89

23: Was hast du gesagt? Wie man mitteilt, was Leute gesagt und wie sie es gesagt haben. 93

24: Wiederholung 97

Nachschlageteil 101

Antwortschlüssel 103

Grammatik auf einen Blick 109

Glossar 115

Einleitung

Dieses *Berlitz-Übungsbuch* ist für all diejenigen gedacht, die genügend Englisch für einfache alltägliche Kommunikation gelernt haben und nun ihr sprachliches Wissen vertiefen und im Umgang mit der Sprache sicherer werden wollen.

Vielleicht besuchen Sie eine Abendschule oder machen ein Selbststudium und benötigen zusätzliche Übung – oder vielleicht haben Sie vor einiger Zeit Englisch gelernt und wollen nun Ihre Sprachkenntnisse auffrischen. Wie dem auch sei, Sie werden feststellen, daß Sie mit dem *Berlitz-Übungsbuch* Ihr Englisch ohne Mühe und auf unterhaltsame Art und Weise verbessern können.

Wie man das *Übungsbuch* benutzt

Wir schlagen vor, daß Sie sich ein wöchentliches oder, falls möglich, tägliches Studienziel setzen, das im Rahmen des Machbaren liegt. Die Lektionen werden zunehmend schwieriger und haben eine fortlaufende Handlung – es ist daher sinnvoll, mit Lektion 1 anzufangen.

Jede Lektion konzentriert sich auf ein spezielles Thema oder eine bestimmte Situation: sich vorstellen; zum Essen ausgehen; Reisen; Hobbys und vieles andere mehr. Die Lektionen selbst enthalten Übungen und Wortpuzzles, die Ihr Vokabular und Ihre Grammatik aufbauen und Ihre Kommunikationsfähigkeit steigern. Die Übungen variieren, doch jede Lektion folgt demselben Grundmuster:

Paare	verhältnismäßig leichte Zuordnungsübungen, die jedes Thema vorstellen
Sprechprobe	verschiedene Übungen, die auf lebhaften, idiomatischen Dialogen beruhen. Lesen Sie diese Dialoge aufmerksam durch, da sie die Sprache vorstellen, die Sie in den darauffolgenden Übungen anwenden
Wortschatztraining	anregende Aktivitäten und Spiele zum Aufbau Ihres Vokabulars
Grammatik im Visier	besondere Übungen, die sich auf Problemzonen der Grammatik konzentrieren
Leseecke	anspruchsvolle, auf einem kurzen Text basierende Übungen zum besseren Verständnis der Sprache
Schreibprobe	kurze Schreibaufgaben, die Schlüsselvokabular und Grammatik der vorhergehenden Übungen verwenden

Wenn Sie die Bedeutung eines englischen Worts nachsehen wollen, finden Sie im Glossar am Ende des *Übungsbuchs* die deutsche Übersetzung. Der Grammatikteil bietet einen Überblick über die in diesem *Übungsbuch* behandelten Hauptthemen. Ihre Antworten können Sie anhand des Antwortschlüssels überprüfen.

Wir wünschen Ihnen viel Erfolg bei Ihrem Studium und hoffen, daß das *Berlitz-Übungsbuch* für Sie nicht nur von praktischem Nutzen ist, sondern Ihnen auch Spaß macht.

Lektion 1: Alles über mich.

In Lektion 1 geht es um Namen und Adresse, um Sichvorstellen und Nationalitäten.

Paare

1. *to be* (sein)

Ordnen Sie die Wörter der passenden Form des Verbs zu.

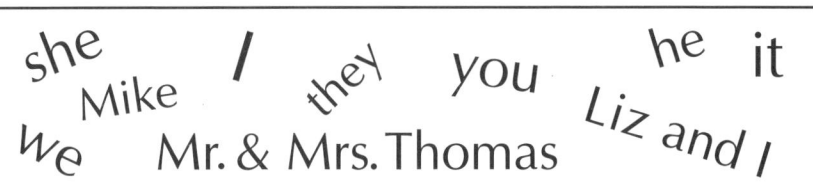

Sprechprobe

2. Sichvorstellen

Dave Burton hat heute morgen ein Vorstellungsgespräch für einen neuen Job. Er ist gerade angekommen. Lesen Sie den Dialog und setzen Sie eines der im Kästchen angegebenen Wörter ein.

are	I'm	isn't	it's	meet	you

Dave   Good morning.
Liz: Good morning! Mr Thomas?
Dave   No, my name _____ Thomas. _____ Burton, Dave Burton.
Liz: Oh, Mr Burton! _____ sorry! How do _____ do? I'm Liz Stones.
Dave   Pleased to _____ you, Ms Stones.
Liz   Coffee? Tea?
Dave   Thank you. Coffee, please.
Liz   Sue! SUE!...SUE? Where _____ you?
Sue   Sorry! Yes?
Liz   Sue, one coffee and one tea, please.

Wortschatztraining

3. Länder und Nationalitäten

Ergänzen Sie die Tabelle.

Country	Nationality
France	French
Spain	
England	
	German
	Scottish
Italy	
the United States	
	Canadian
Japan	
	Indian
Australia	

4. Zahlen

Stellen Sie die Buchstaben um, um die Zahlen zu finden, und ordnen Sie dann die Zahlen den Wörtern zu.

herte _____

ixs _*six*_

veens _____

net _____

wot _____

eon _____

enni _____

rufo _____

thige _____

vief _____

Grammatik im Visier

5. Kurzformen

Schreiben Sie wie im Beispiel gezeigt die Kurzformen von *is, are* und *am*.

Beispiel: He is Spanish. — He's Spanish.

1. His name is Dave Burton.
2. They are from France.
3. What is your name?
4. I am Liz Stones.
5. We are American.
6. It is coffee.
7. She is my girlfriend.
8. Where is my tea?

6. Verneinung

Schauen Sie sich die Bilder an und bilden Sie Sätze wie im Beispiel. Verwenden Sie die Kurzformen.

Beipiel: He isn't Mr. Kushner.
He's Mr Thomas.

1. _____ She's Spanish.
2. _____ They're from Canada.
3. _____ It's tea.
4. Her name _____ It's James.
5. _____ I'm married.

Leseecke

7. Personal information

Sehen Sie sich die Informationen auf Daves Bewerbungsformular an. Bringen Sie anschließend die Zeilen in die richtige Reihenfolge und schreiben Sie die Sätze hin.

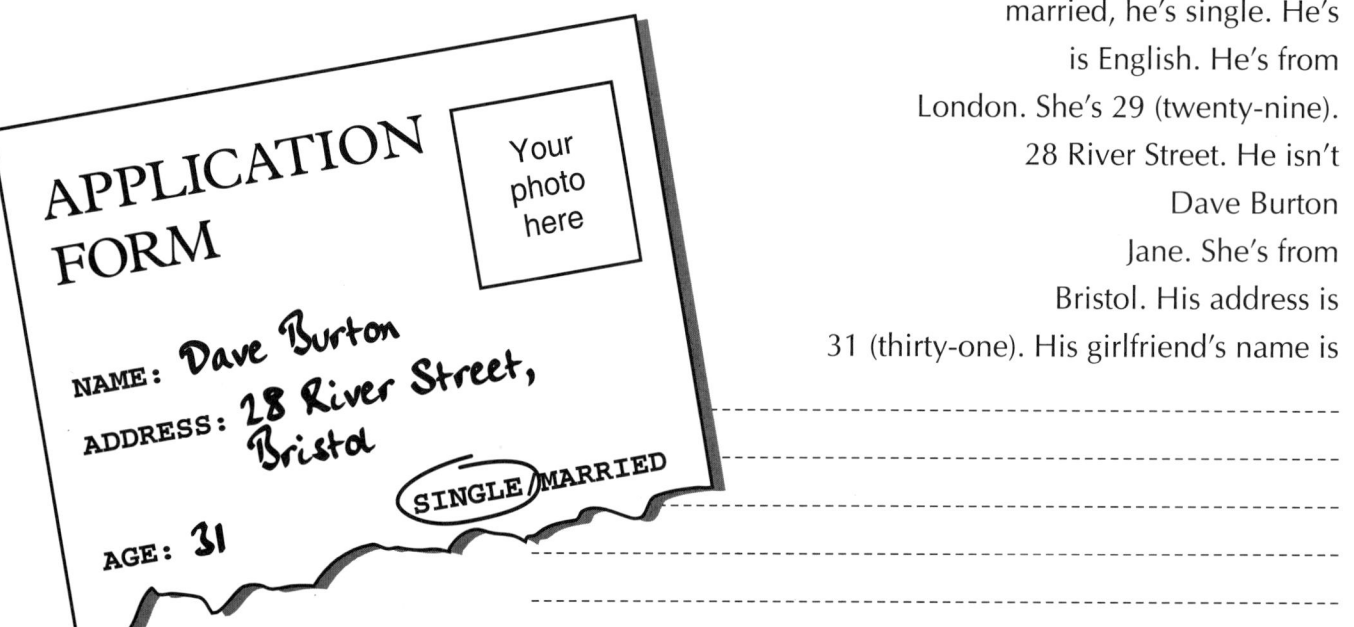

married, he's single. He's
is English. He's from
London. She's 29 (twenty-nine).
28 River Street. He isn't
Dave Burton
Jane. She's from
Bristol. His address is
31 (thirty-one). His girlfriend's name is

Schreibprobe

8. Alles über Sie

Schreiben Sie Sätze über sich selbst.

Beispiel: (name) *My name is Liz Stones.*

Personal Information

(name) _____
(address) _____
_____
(nationality) _____
(age) _____
(married/single) _____

Lektion 2: Ich habe einen neuen Job.

In Lektion 2 üben Sie, wie man über die Familie spricht, wie man Fragen übers Alter stellt und wie man über seinen Job spricht.

Paare

1. Questions and answers

Ordnen Sie jede Frage der passenden Antwort zu.
Achtung: Es gibt eine Antwort zuviel.

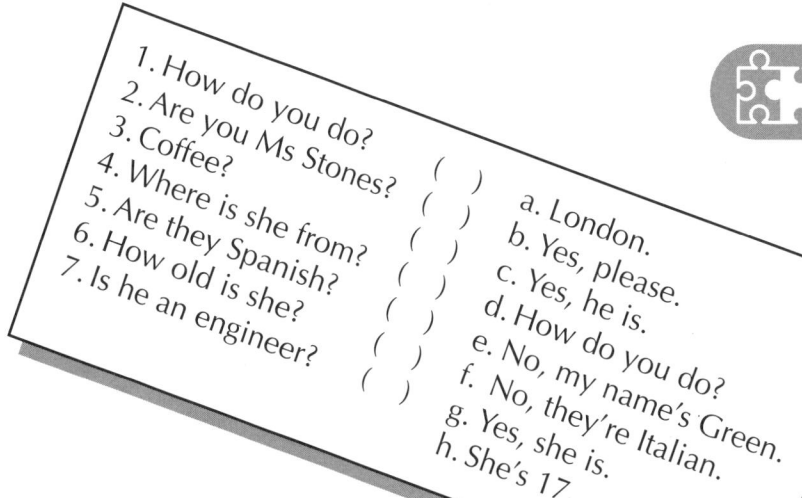

1. How do you do?
2. Are you Ms Stones?
3. Coffee?
4. Where is she from?
5. Are they Spanish?
6. How old is she?
7. Is he an engineer?

( )
( )
( )
( )
( )
( )
( )

a. London.
b. Yes, please.
c. Yes, he is.
d. How do you do?
e. No, my name's Green.
f. No, they're Italian.
g. Yes, she is.
h. She's 17.

Sprechprobe

2. *a* oder *an*?

Daves Vorstellungsgespräch war erfolgreich. Von zu Hause ruft er seine Freundin Jane an, um ihr die Neuigkeit mitzuteilen. Füllen Sie die Lücken in ihrer Unterhaltung mit *a* oder *an*.

Jane	Hello?
Dave	Hi, it's Dave.
Jane	Oh, hi Dave.
Dave	Hey, I've got _____ job! I've got _____ new job!
Jane	You've got _____ new job? Where?
Dave	Walker International. It's _____ travel company - _____ international travel company. I'm _____ travel reporter!
Jane	You're not _____ reporter. You're _____ engineer!
Dave	Ah, I'm _____ reporter *now*!
Jane	I see.
Dave	I've got _____ job, and _____ office, and _____ nice boss.
Jane	What's his name?
Dave	Her name is Stones. Her first name is Liz. Liz Stones
Jane	*Her* name? Your boss is _____ woman? How old is she? Where is she from? Is she single?
Dave	Hey, it's okay! She's married. She's got _____ husband and she's got four children.

Wortschatztraining

3. How old are you?

Werfen Sie einen Blick auf die Tabelle und vervollständigen Sie die Sätze.

NAME	AGE
John	24
Jane	29
Sue	32
Peter	32
Mary	59
Tony	62
Alice	81

John is twenty-four.

Jane

Sue and Peter

Mary

Tony

Alice

4. Janes Familie

Schauen Sie sich die Wörter im Kästchen an und schreiben Sie ein W neben die, die weiblich sind, und ein M neben die, die männlich sind. Sehen Sie sich dann Janes Stammbaum an und ergänzen Sie die nachfolgenden Sätze.

grandfather ----
grandmother ----
father ----
mother ----
sister ----
brother ----
son ----
daughter ----
uncle ----
aunt ----
niece ----
nephew ----
husband ----
wife ----

1. My brother's name is _____
2. My _____ 's name is Sue.
3. Sue is married. Her _____ 's name is Peter.
4. Their daughter's name is _____
5. Their _____ 's name is Tom.

6. Jenny is my _____, and Tom is my _____
7. My _____ 's name is Mary, and my _____ 's name is Tony.
8. My _____ 's name is Alice.

Grammatik im Visier

5. have got

Sehen Sie sich nochmals Janes Stammbaum an und vervollständigen Sie die folgenden Sätze.

Beispiel: Sue and Peter **have got two** children.

1. John _____ sisters.
2. Jenny _____ brother.
3. Jane _____ niece and one nephew.
4. Mary and Tony _____ children.
5. Jenny and Tom _____ aunts.
6. Alice _____ grandchildren.

6. Fragen bilden

Hier finden Sie die Antworten auf einige Fragen. Bilden Sie Fragen aus den Wörtern.

Beispiel: address/is/Dave's/what   F. **What is Dave's address?**
A. It's 28 River Street, Bristol.

1. you/car/got/have/a   F. _____ ?
A. Yes, I have.

2. John/a/got/has/girlfriend   F. _____ ?
A. No, he hasn't.

3. Mr/from/Thomas/where/and/Mrs/are   F. _____ ?
A. From New York.

4. boss's/your/is/what/name   F. _____ ?
A. It's Liz Stones.

5. old/are/children/Sue's/how   F. _____ ?
A. Four and seven.

6. husband's/is/what/job/her   F. _____ ?
A. He's an accountant.

Leseecke

7. Dear Mum, ...

Lesen Sie Daves Nachricht an seine Eltern und antworten Sie auf die Aussagen, wie im Beispiel gezeigt.

> DEAR MUM AND DAD,
> HOW ARE YOU? I'M FINE. GOOD NEWS - I'VE GOT A NEW JOB! I'M NOT AN ENGINEER NOW - I'M A REPORTER. I'M A REPORTER, A TRAVEL REPORTER. IT'S A BIG COMPANY - IT'S GOT BRANCHES IN PARIS, ROME, NEW YORK, MADRID, BERLIN - AND TOKYO!! OH, AND ITS NAME IS WALKER INTERNATIONAL.
> LOVE, Dave
> P.S. I'VE GOT A NEW GIRLFRIEND, TOO. HER NAME IS JANE, AND SHE'S FROM LONDON. SHE'S A PHOTOGRAPHER.

Beispiel: Dave has got bad news. *No, he hasn't. He's got good news*

1. Dave has got a new car.
2. Dave is an engineer now.
3. Walker International is a small company.
4. It has got five branches.
5. Dave's girlfriend is a reporter.

Schreibprobe

8. Die Fragen des Polizisten

Auf dem Nachhauseweg vom Büro wird Liz von einem Polizisten angehalten, der ihr eine Menge Fragen stellt. Vervollständigen Sie die Unterhaltung, indem Sie die Fragen und Antworten einsetzen.

Policeman Excuse me.
Liz Yes?
Policeman (Mrs Liz Jones?) *Are you Mrs Liz Jones?*
Liz (no - Liz Stones) *No, I'm not. I'm Liz Stones.*
Policeman (address 47 Elm Avenue?)
Liz (no - 47 Oak Avenue)
Policeman (married?)
Liz (yes)
Policeman (husband's name?)
Liz (Philip)
Policeman (accountant?)
Liz (no - teacher)
Policeman (from Paris?)
Liz (no - Scottish)
Policeman Oh, I see. I'm sorry. I'm very sorry. Mistake! Goodbye!

Lektion 3: Wo ist Ihr Büro?

In dieser Lektion befassen wir uns mit Beschreibungen, mit Häusern, Büros und Hotels samt ihren Einrichtungen und mit Farben.

Paare

1. Wo ist die Katze?

Ordnen Sie die Bilder den Ausdrücken zu.

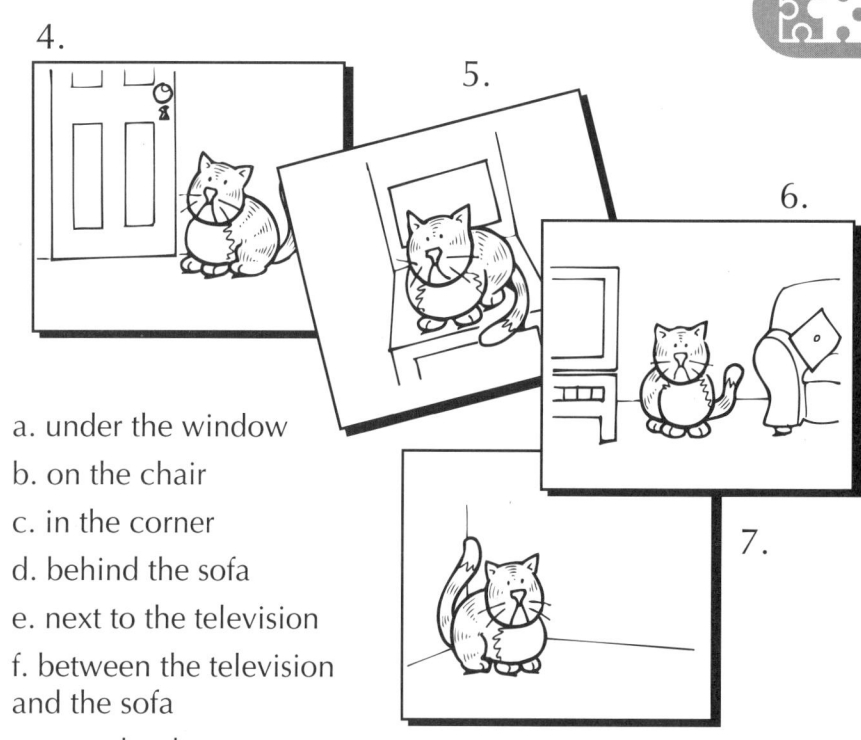

a. under the window
b. on the chair
c. in the corner
d. behind the sofa
e. next to the television
f. between the television and the sofa
g. near the door

Sprechprobe

2. About the office

Dave telefoniert mit seiner Mutter und erzählt ihr von seinem neuen Job bei Walker International. Vervollständigen Sie die Unterhaltung, indem Sie den geeignetsten Ausdruck in die Lücken einsetzen.

Mother   Where is the company, Dave?

Dave   It's (in/on) _____ Greenwood. It's the big white building, next to the Fairview Hotel.

Mother   Oh, yes. And how many people (is/are) _____ there in Walker International?

Dave   (There/They) _____ are fifty-three people in the Greenwood branch.

Mother	(Have/Has) _____ you got an office?
Dave	Yes, I have. But there are five people in it, so there are five computers, five desks, five chairs and five telephones too - and it's a small office! And it's got pink (door/doors) _____ and a pink carpet. But it's nice - there's a big window, and there's a park (behind/next) _____ the building.
Mother	Are there any women in your office?
Dave	Yes, there are (one/two) _____ women.
Mother	And are there any shops (near/next) _____ the office? Or restaurants?
Dave	Yes, there's an Italian restaurant. And there's a small sandwich shop (behind/between) _____ the hotel.

Wortschatztraining

3. Farben

Im Wortquadrat sind elf Farben versteckt. Können Sie sie finden? Eine Farbe ist schon angegeben.

```
T G Y E L L O W S S
R E R E D D E H P O
W R P A O B G A I L
H Y P E Y S R T N O
I B U B L U E R K Y
T L R C E D E N Y T
E A P O R A N G E S
S C L O W M R O M P
O K E L L N M F Y F
P E S U T H W E G E
```

4. Was ist überzählig?

Machen Sie einen Kreis um das Wort, das nicht zur angegebenen Wortgruppe paßt.

1. **office**: desk shop chair computer telephone boss
2. **living room**: sofa carpet chair toilet television table
3. **kitchen**: lobby fridge washing machine knife sink window
4. **bathroom**: sink bath shower soap egg door
5. **house**: bedroom toilet garage garden bathroom gym

Grammatik im Visier

5. a/an/some/any

Füllen Sie die Lücken mit *a, an, some* oder *any*.

1. There are _____ shops and restaurants near the office.
2. My sister has got _____ red sports car.
3. Are there _____ hotels in Greenwood?

4. Is there _____ swimming pool in this hotel?
5. There aren't _____ eggs in the fridge.
6. There are _____ French and German people in the lobby.
7. Has Dave got _____ brothers and sisters?
8. Is there _____ orange umbrella under the table?

6. Fragen und Antworten bilden

Stellen Sie mit den angegebenen Hinweisen einige Fragen und geben Sie kurze Antworten.

Beispiel: sofa/living room — Is there a sofa in the living room?
Yes, there is

1. shower/bathroom _____
   Yes,

2. washing machine/kitchen _____
   No,

3. eggs/fridge _____
   Yes,

4. restaurants/Greenwood _____
   Yes,

5. women/your office _____
   No,

6. pink carpet/living room _____
   Yes,

Leseecke

7. *The Fairview Hotel*

Lesen Sie die Beschreibung darüber, wie das Parterre des Hotels Fairview angelegt ist, und schreiben Sie dann die Lage der verschiedenen Einrichtungen auf den Plan.

There is a large French restaurant next to the lobby on the left, and there's a small coffee shop next to the lobby on the right. There's a book shop between the coffee shop and the travel office. The public telephones are near the travel office. There's a small gym next to the sauna, and a small swimming pool behind the gym. There are toilets in the corner near the restaurant. In the corner of the lobby there are some sofas, chairs and coffee tables.

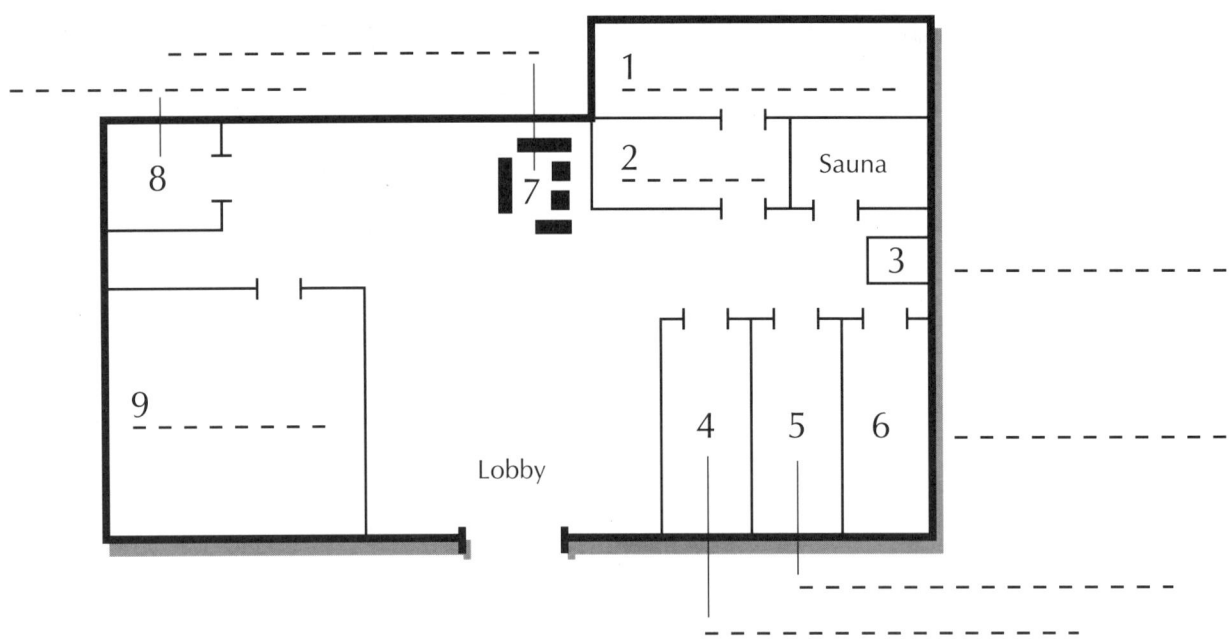

 # Schreibprobe

8. Janes neues Haus

Daves Freundin Jane ist kürzlich in ein neues Haus eingezogen. Lesen Sie die Beschreibung und beantworten Sie dann die folgenden Fragen.

Beispiel: _Is there a shower?_
No, there isn't.

1. _____
There are two.

2. _____
Yes, there is. It's in the kitchen.

3. _____
It's yellow.

4. _____
It's next to the house.

5. _____
Yes, there are three apple trees.

6. _____
It's behind the house.

GREAT VALUE!!!!
small house, 2 bedrooms, bathroom (no shower), large kitchen with washing machine, yellow living room!!, garage (next to house), small garden behind house (3 apple trees).
Please call 213-444-3321.

Lektion 4: Liebst du mich?

Hier geht um das, was man mag und was man nicht mag, um Uhrzeit, Sport und Hobbys.

Paare

1. Reimwörter

Verbinden Sie die Wörter, die sich reimen.

Sprechprobe

2. Breakfast time

Liz Stones hat gerade das Frühstück zubereitet und wartet nun darauf, daß ihre Kinder Linda und James und ihr Mann Philip nach unten kommen. Lesen Sie die Unterhaltung und beantworten Sie die Fragen.

Liz Breakfast! Breakfast time! Where are they? Where are the children? Breakfast is ready!

Philip Breakfast is ready, but the children aren't. Linda is still in the bath, and James is still in bed. And he's got my newspaper.

Liz What?! But it's 8:00 (eight o'clock) ! It's late. Breakfast is on the table.

Philip I'm ready. Bacon and sausages - good. I love bacon and sausages. Ah, here's Linda.

Linda Morning mum, morning dad.

Liz You're late - it's 8:00. And now I'm late, and your father's late, too.

Linda Sorry. Is this my breakfast? Bacon and sausages? Oh, yuk! No, thank you.

Liz What? But you like bacon and sausages!

Linda No, I don't. I don't like meat. I hate meat! I'm a vegetarian.

Liz You? You're not a vegetarian.

Linda Yes, I am. I'm a vegetarian now. Is there any coffee?

Beispiel: Who's in the bath? _Linda is in the bath._

1. Who's still in bed?
2. Who has got Philip's newspaper?
3. Who's ready?
4. Who likes bacon and sausages?
5. Who doesn't like meat?
6. Who's a vegetarian?

Wortschatztraining

3. Wieviel Uhr ist es?

Schreiben Sie die entsprechende Uhrzeit unter jede Uhr.

Beispiel:

1. _____ 2. _____

It's half past nine.   3. _____   4. _____

4. Wo ist er um 7:00?

Bilden Sie Sätze über Daves Tagesplan unter Verwendung der Ausdrücke im Kasten.

Beispiel: 7:00 _At seven o'clock he's in bed._

1. 7:30
2. 8:30
3. 9:00
4. 1:00
5. 6:30
6. 8:30

> the sandwich shop
> in the bath
> in the pub
> in bed
> in his car
> in his office
> in the gym

5. Like it or hate it?

Schreiben Sie diese Sätze nach dem Grad des Mögens um.

1. I quite like it. __I love it.__
2. I hate it. _____
3. I like it very much. _____
4. I don't like it very much. _____
5. It's okay. _____
6. I love it. _____
7. I don't like it at all. _____

Grammatik im Visier

6. Do you love me?

Wählen Sie das passende Wort für die Lücken.

1. I don't like my job at all. In fact, I hate _____
2. Do you like cats? Yes, I love _____
3. My boss's name is Liz Stones - I quite like _____
4. I like Uncle John, but my husband doesn't like _____ at all
5. I love Pete, but he doesn't love _____
6. Where's my umbrella? Liz, have you got _____ ?
7. We don't like our new teacher, and she doesn't like _____ !
8. A new sports car!! Thank you, Dad. I love _____ !

> me you him her it them us

7. Kurze Antworten

Geben Sie wie im Beispiel kurze Antworten auf die folgenden Fragen.

Beispiel: Is it 10:00? Yes, __it is.__

1. Is Linda still in the bath? Yes, _____
2. Does your daughter like her new teacher? No, _____
3. Sorry, Mum - am I late? No, _____
4. Do you like red wine? Yes, _____
5. Are you a vegetarian? Yes, _____
6. Do they like London? No, _____

Leseecke

8. She likes red wine, but...

Dave ist sich über seine Freundin Jane nicht ganz im klaren, weil sie beide einen so unterschiedlichen Geschmack haben. Lesen Sie diesen Teil des Briefs an einen Freund und bringen Sie die Sätze in die richtige Reihenfolge.

a. meat, but she's a vegetarian. She
b. like it very much. She likes swimming and
c. She likes red wine, but
d. loves shopping, but I hate it.
e. I like beer. I love
f. I like dancing, but she doesn't
g. like her? Yes, I do.
h. badminton, but I don't. Do I

Schreibprobe

9. Do you like dancing?

Am Samstag trifft Liz Stones ihre Freunde Pete und Jenny, und gemeinsam überlegen sie, was sie unternehmen sollen. Stellen Sie Fragen darüber, was die drei gern machen, und beantworten Sie sie.

	Pete	Liz	Jenny	you
badminton	very much!	not very much	not at all	?
shopping	hate it	not really	love it!	?
dancing	it's okay	Yuk!!! hate it	no!!! hate it	?
pubs	love them	like them	not really	?

Beispiel: Pete/badminton
F. Does Pete like badminton?
A. Yes, he does. He likes it very much.

1. Jenny/shopping? F. _____ A. _____
2. Liz and Jenny/dancing? F. _____ A. _____
3. Jenny/badminton? F. _____ A. _____
4. Pete/pubs? F. _____ A. _____
5. you/badminton? shopping? dancing? pubs? F. _____ A. _____

Lektion 5: Sind Sie morgen abend frei?

In dieser Lektion geht es um tägliche Aktivitäten und darum, wie oft man etwas tut. Dazu weitere Übungen zur Uhrzeit und zu den Wochentagen.

Paare

1. Wieviel Uhr ist es?

Ordnen Sie die Uhren der richtigen Uhrzeit zu.

1. quarter past seven
2. quarter past three
3. four fifteen
4. quarter to four
5. nine forty-five
6. eight fifteen
7. quarter to twelve
8. quarter to one

Sprechprobe

2. How about a date?

Es ist Daves zweite Woche in seinem neuen Job. Er begrüßt Anne, die Empfangsdame, als er am Montagmorgen ankommt. Setzen Sie das richtige Verb aus dem Kasten in die Lücken.

eat   watch   play(x2)   meet(x2)   cook   learn(x2)   visit   read

Anne Morning, Dave.

Dave Morning, Anne. Ummm… Anne? Are you busy this evening? I'm free, so…

Anne Sorry, Dave. I _____ tennis on Mondays. I always _____ tennis on Mondays.

Dave I see. How about tomorrow? Are you free tomorrow evening?

Anne That's Tuesday. No, I'm sorry, but I _____ Spanish on Tuesdays. And I _____ the guitar on Wednesdays.

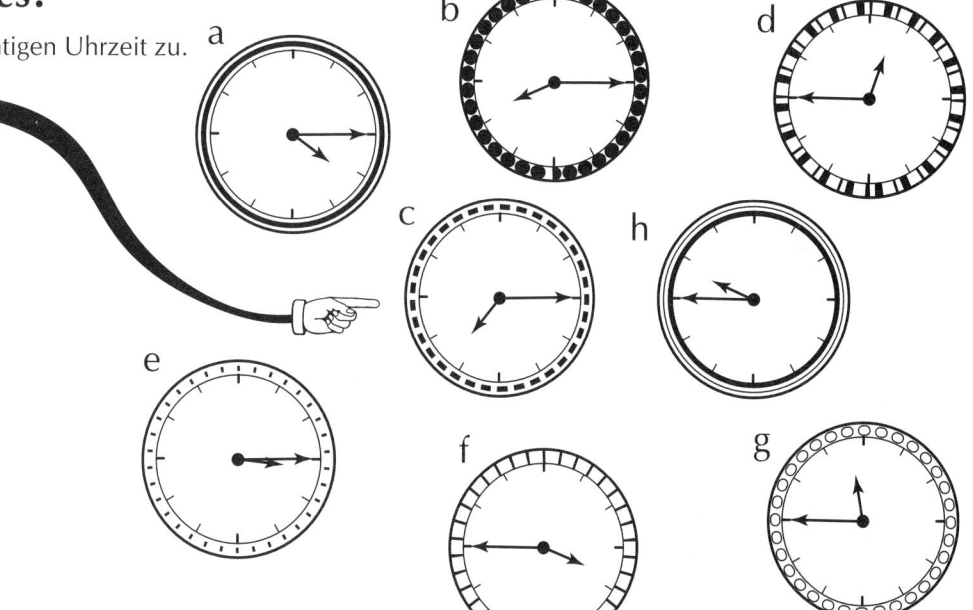

Dave	Hmmm. This is difficult. What do you do on Thursdays and Fridays? Do you _____ Japanese poetry? Do you _____ Chinese food?
Anne	No, I don't. I usually _____ TV at home on Thursdays, and I always _____ my parents on Fridays, and _____ dinner at their house.
Dave	And the weekend? How about Saturday and Sunday?
Anne	I never _____ strange men at the weekend.
Dave	I'm not strange! I'm Dave!
Anne	Sorry, but I always _____ my boyfriend at the weekend. And you've got a girlfriend, Dave.

Wortschatztraining

3. Das Verb finden

Finden Sie das passende Verb für jedes Bild.

Beispiel:

drink

a. _____
b. _____
c. _____
d. _____
e. _____
f. _____

4. Tägliche Aktivitäten

Schreiben Sie die Zahlen 1 bis 11 neben die Tätigkeiten, und zwar in der Reihenfolge, in der Sie sie ausführen. Markieren Sie dann die Zeit auf der 24-Stunden-Uhr.

_____ read the newspaper
_____ eat breakfast
_____ cook dinner

_____ go to bed
_____ have a shower/bath
_____ start work
_____ get up
_____ finish work
_____ watch TV
_____ go to work
_____ have lunch

Grammatik im Visier

5. Verdrehte Sätze

Bringen Sie die Wörter in die richtige Reihenfolge.

1. football   always   Saturdays   I   on   play

   ----

2. parents   visits   Anne   her   often

   ----

3. Dave   his   work   to   usually   car   drives

   ----

4. red   often   drink   don't   wine   I

   ----

5. Fridays   Liz   gym   to   sometimes   goes   the   on

   ----

6. meat   eats   Linda   never

   ----

6. Fragen bilden

Ergänzen Sie die Sätze mit *do* oder *does* und einer kurzen Antwort, wie im Beispiel gezeigt.

   Beispiel: Does she always get up at 7:15? Yes, **she does.**

1. _____ the children like their new school? Yes, _____ .
2. _____ he work in London? No, _____ .
3. _____ you often write letters? No, _____ .
4. _____ your parents live in Oxford? Yes, _____ .
5. _____ your sister eat meat? No, _____ .
6. _____ you drive a car? Yes, _____ .

Leseecke

7. Janes Tagebuch

Daves Freundin Jane findet das Leben langweilig. Sie meint, es sei Zeit für eine Veränderung. Lesen Sie ihr Tagebuch und setzen Sie *to, at, on* oder *in* in die Lücken ein.

MONDAY

My life isn't interesting at all. I always get up _____ 7:15. I always go _____ work _____ 8:30 and I always come home _____ 6:00. I read the newspaper, I watch TV, I write letters and _____ my friend _____ Spain, _____ my family. I usually meet friends _____ Saturday and Sunday, and we usually play tennis _____ Greenwood. I always meet Dave, too. Sometimes we go _____ a restaurant and sometimes we go _____ a pub. But I always meet the same people. It's always the same.......

Schreibprobe

8. Über Sie

Beantworten Sie diese Fragen über sich selbst.

1. Where do you live?   _____
2. Do you often play tennis?   _____
3. What time do you usually get up?   _____
4. What time do you usually have lunch?   _____
5. What do you usually do on Sunday?   _____
6. Do you drive a car?   _____

Lektion 6: Wieviel kostet das?

In dieser Lektion geht es ums Einkaufen: Sie üben, wie man nach verschiedenen Artikeln, Preisen und Größen fragt. Außerdem finden Sie Vokabular über Kleidung.

Paare

1. Beim Einkaufen

Ordnen Sie die Satzenden den Satzanfängen zu.

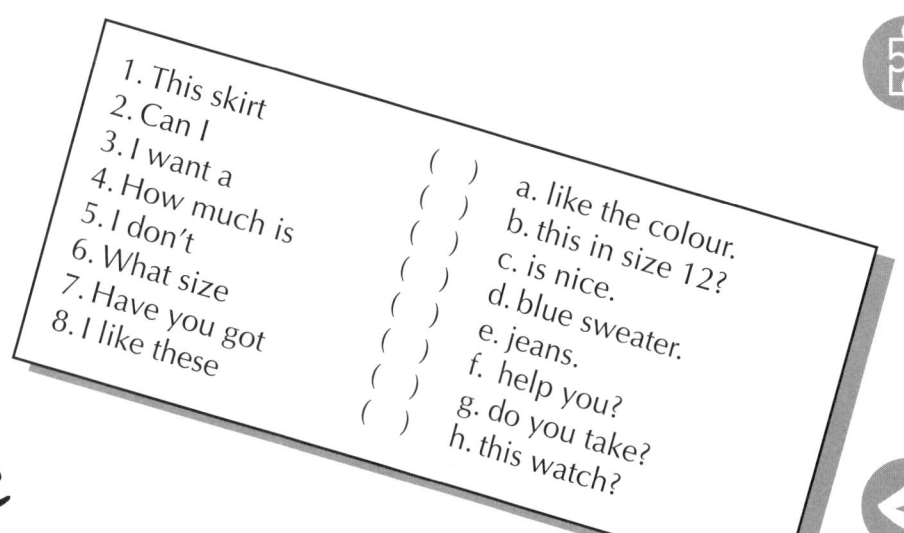

1. This skirt
2. Can I
3. I want a
4. How much is
5. I don't
6. What size
7. Have you got
8. I like these

( ) a. like the colour.
( ) b. this in size 12?
( ) c. is nice.
( ) d. blue sweater.
( ) e. jeans.
( ) f. help you?
( ) g. do you take?
( ) h. this watch?

Sprechprobe

2. Dave's birthday present

Dave hat bald Geburtstag, und Jane ist mit ihrer Freundin Pat unterwegs, um ein Geschenk zu kaufen. Lesen Sie die Unterhaltung und beantworten Sie die Fragen.

Pat This shirt is nice.

Jane Yes, it is, but Dave doesn't like brown.

Pat What colours does he usually wear?

Jane He likes blue or grey or black. Sometimes he wears green.

Pat How about this one? It's a nice colour.

Jane What size is it? Medium. How much is it? Where's the label?

Pat Here it is. What!? £55.00 (fifty-five pounds)!?

Jane It's silk. I don't like that price at all.

Clerk Good morning. Can I help you?

Jane Yes, please. I want a cotton shirt, in blue or grey. A casual shirt. It's for my boyfriend.

Clerk What size does he take?

Jane I don't know. Medium, maybe.

Clerk These shirts are very popular now. Or these?

Jane They're nice. How much are they?

Clerk	They're £35.00.
Jane	What? £35.00? I haven't got £35.00!
Pat	How about a tie? These are cheap.
Jane	Good idea. I don't want an expensive present. I don't like Dave very much now. A cheap tie is a good idea.

1. What colours does Dave like? _____

2. Does he like brown? _____

3. How much is the silk shirt? _____

4. Does Jane want a cotton shirt or a silk shirt? _____

5. Has she got £35.00? _____

6. Does she know Dave's size? _____

Wortschatztraining

3. Die Kleider finden

Ordnen Sie die Buchstaben, um die Kleidungsstücke zu finden.

Beispiel: resed   _dress_

1. trish   _____
2. trawees   _____
3. cossk   _____
4. trisk   _____
5. ite   _____

6. janes   _____
7. hoses   _____
8. catkej   _____
9. sluboe   _____
10. toca   _____

4. *Money, money, money*

Schreiben Sie die folgenden Preise voll aus.

Beispiel: £3.50   _three (pounds) fifty_

1. £7.00   _____
2. £1.45   _____
3. £4.99   _____
4. £6.50   _____

5. £15.00 _____
6. £49.99 _____
7. £125.00 _____
8. £500.00 _____

Grammatik im Visier

5. do, don't, does, doesn't...

Füllen Sie die Lücken mit *do/don't, does/doesn't, is/isn't* oder *are/aren't*.

1. Excuse me, how much _____ these gloves?
2. _____ you have this skirt in green?
3. What colour _____ you want?
4. I'm sorry, I _____ want a medium, I want a large.
5. _____ this silk or cotton?
6. What size _____ he take?
7. This bag _____ nice - how much is it?
8. These shoes _____ my size - they're size 6. Have you got size 7?

6. How much is it?

Stellen Sie nach dem Beispiel Fragen zu den gezeigten Gegenständen und beantworten Sie die Fragen.

Beispiel:

F: How much are these gloves?
A: They're five (pounds) ninety-nine.

£5.99

1. £35.00

2. £9.50

3. £24.99

4. 50p

5. £7.50

6. £2.50

Leseecke

7. Wer kocht?

Lesen Sie die Beschreibung und ergänzen Sie den Text mit der richtigen Form der Verben aus dem Kästchen.

**hate
eat (x2)
go (x2)
buy
like (x3)
come
cook (x2)**

Liz _____ shopping, but she _____ cooking. Her husband, Philip, _____ cooking, but doesn't _____ shopping very much. So Liz usually _____ to the supermarket after work, and _____ food for dinner. Then Philip _____ home at about 6.30, and _____ dinner. (This is sometimes difficult - their daughter Linda doesn't _____ meat, and their son James doesn't _____ fish.) At the weekend, sometimes the children _____ , and sometimes they all _____ to a restaurant for dinner. This is expensive - but it's easy.

Schreibprobe

8. Fragen zum Thema Einkauf

Bilden Sie geeignete Fragen, die zu diesen Antworten passen.

Beispiel: *Have you got any silk shirts?*
No, I'm sorry. We haven't got any silk shirts.

1. _____
   She takes a size 12.

2. _____
   It's £35.00.

3. _____
   It's black and grey.

4. _____
   They're 25 pence.

5. _____
   Yes, please. Do you have any cotton socks?

6. _____
   The ties? They're next to the shirts.

Lektion 7: Die Kneipe ist dort unten.

Lektion 7 behandelt Richtungen, Geschäfte und öffentliche Gebäude und Öffnungszeiten.

Paare

1. *It's on the left.*

Ordnen Sie die Beschreibungen den Bildern zu.

1. opposite
2. third house on the right
3. straight ahead
4. on the left
5. straight on at the crossroads
6. on the right
7. second house on the left
8. at the end

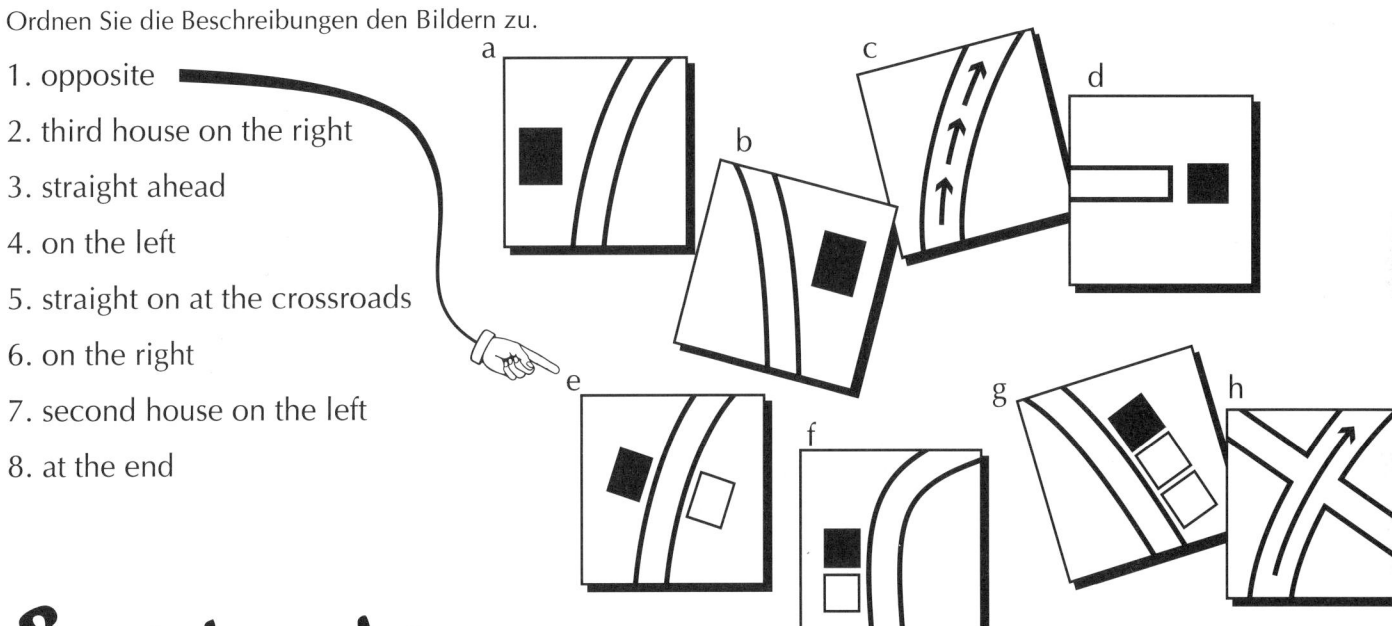

Sprechprobe

2. Wie komme ich nach …?

Dave ist unterwegs, um seine Freundin Jane zu treffen. Sie wollen etwas trinken gehen, aber er ist spät dran. Als er die Straße entlangeilt, hält ihn eine junge Japanerin, eine Touristin, an.

Tourist Excuse me…

Dave Yes, can I help you?

Tourist Is the Victoria Art Gallery (far/near) _____ here?

Dave It's not far. Do you (know/see) _____ the post office on that corner? Turn left (here/there) _____ - that's Baker Street. Go (under/over) _____ the river bridge, and then go straight along Baker Street until you come to a big church (on/at) _____ your right. Turn right there, and the Victoria Art Gallery is on (your/my) _____ left. There's a big sign (inside/outside) _____. You can't miss it.

Tourist I'm sorry... Do I turn left (or/and) _____ right at the post office? And where is the river bridge? I'm sorry, I don't understand.

Dave Okay, come with (I/me) _____. (Dave goes with her.) Here is the post office. Turn left here. Now, here is the river bridge. By the way, (where/here) _____ are you from?

Tourist I'm from Japan. (She sees Jane across the road.) Excuse me, that woman... is she your friend?

Jane Hey!

Dave Jane! It's Jane, my girlfriend. Er, um, hello!

Jane Hello, Dave. And (who/what) _____ is this? Your new girlfriend? The pub isn't this way - it's that way.

Dave I know, I know, but...

Jane Okay, you go that way - with your new friend. Goodbye!

Wortschatz-training

3. Zahlen

Füllen Sie das Kreuzworträtsel mit den Ordnungszahlen (*first, second* usw.) aus.

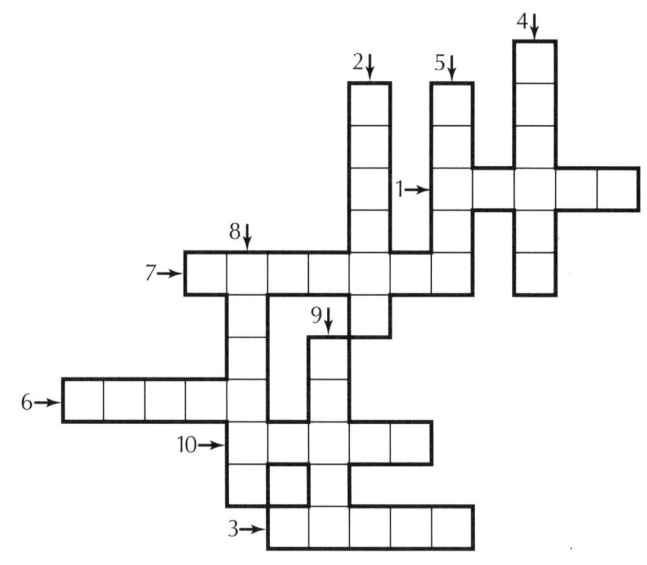

4. Auf der Straße

Wählen Sie zur Ergänzung der Sätze jeweils eines der Wörter aus dem Kästchen.

1. You borrow books from a   _____
2. You buy stamps at a   _____
3. You swim in a   _____
4. You borrow money from a   _____
5. You buy food at a   _____
6. You buy meat at a   _____
7. You eat a meal at a   _____
8. You have a drink at a   _____

post office   bank   supermarket   butcher's   library   pub   restaurant   swimming pool

Grammatik im Visier

5. *to, at* oder *on*?

Füllen Sie die Lücken mit *to, at* oder *on*.

1. The children's department is _____ the third floor.
2. Go straight _____ , until you come to a telephone box.
3. Turn left _____ the church.
4. Our house is second _____ the right.
5. Which floor is Dave's office _____ ?
6. The swimming pool closes _____ 5.30 _____ Sundays.
7. The post office is _____ Broad Street.
8. Our house is _____ the end of the street.

6. Wortfolge

Bringen Sie die Wörter in die richtige Reihenfolge, damit Sie Sätze erhalten.

1. me   is   there   telephone   excuse   here   a   box   near

   -- ?

2. on   fourth   clothes   are   men's   floor   the

   ----

3. closes   Sundays   the   past   ten   half   pub   on   at

   ----

4. right   big   turn   by   the   hotel

   ----

5. is   from   o'clock   library   the   open   nine   weekdays   on

   ----

6. isn't   from   house   far   my   here

Leseecke

7. Where's the party?

Liz Stones hat mehrere Mitarbeiter von Walker International zu einer Party bei sich zu Hause eingeladen. Lesen Sie ihre Anweisungen, wie man zu ihrem Haus gelangt, und markieren Sie die Stellen dann auf der Karte.

Turn left at the crossroads, and go along the road to Whitecross. Take the second right into Forest Drive. Go straight ahead, over the river bridge, until you come to a telephone box on the left. Turn left here, and our house is the second on the right.

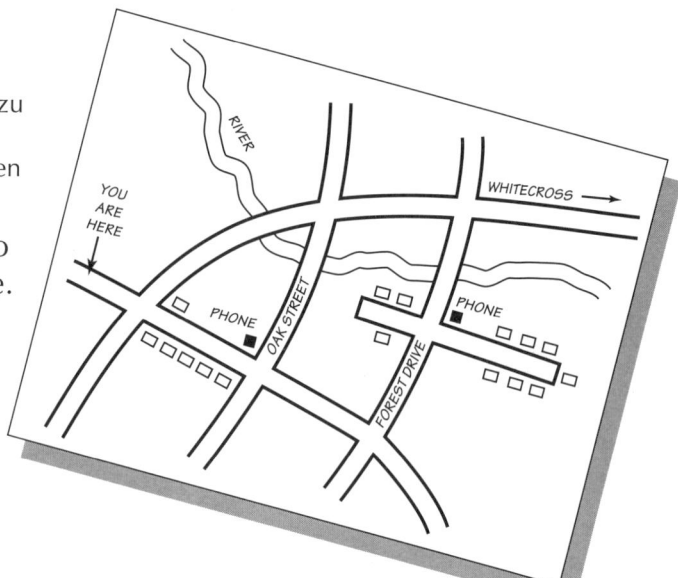

Schreibprobe

8. When is it open?

Sehen Sie sich die Öffnungszeiten an und bilden Sie Fragen und Antworten wie im Beispiel.

Beispiel:

SWIMMING POOL
Opening Times
Tue-Fri: 9:00-7:00
Sat-Sun: 10:00-5:30
(CLOSED MONDAYS)

F. When is the pool open?

A. It's open from nine o'clock to seven o'clock on weekdays, and from ten o'clock to half past five on Sundays. It's closed on Mondays.

Greenwood Library
Monday-Friday 10:00-6:00
Saturday 10:00-5:00
Sunday CLOSED

POST OFFICE

M	9:00	5:30
T	9:00	5:30
W	9:00	5:30
Th	9:00	5:30
F	9:00	5:30
S	9:00	12:30
S	CLOSED	

Casa Fina
Open 6:30 - 11:00
(6:30 - 11:30 on Saturday)
Closed Tue and Sun

1. **F:** _____
   A: _____

2. **F:** _____
   A: _____

3. **F:** _____
   A: _____

Lektion 8: Wie war das Wochenende?

Lektion 8 befaßt sich mit Ereignissen, die in der Vergangenheit geschehen sind, und mit Wochenendaktivitäten. Sie lernen, Fragen zu stellen, die mit *what?, where?, when?* und *who?* beginnen.

Paare

1. Verben

Ordnen Sie den Verben im Präteritum auf der linken Seite ein passendes Wort oder einen Ausdruck auf der rechten Seite zu.

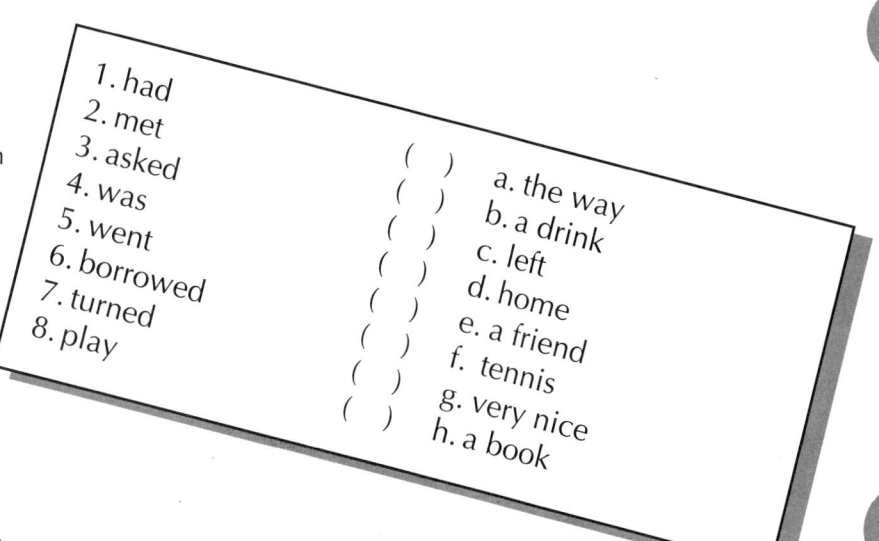

1. had
2. met
3. asked
4. was
5. went
6. borrowed
7. turned
8. play

( ) a. the way
( ) b. a drink
( ) c. left
( ) d. home
( ) e. a friend
( ) f. tennis
( ) g. very nice
( ) h. a book

Sprechprobe

2. How was the weekend?

Am Montagmorgen spricht Dave in der Firma mit Anne, der Empfangsdame, über sein Wochenende. Setzen Sie die richtige Verbform in die Lücken ein.

Anne   How (be) was your weekend, Dave?

Dave   Not good, not good at all.

Anne   Why? What (happen) _____ ?

Dave   Jane and I (have) _____ an argument on Saturday.

Anne   Oh, I see. Why did you (have) _____ an argument?

Dave   She (see) _____ me with another woman.

Anne   Dave!

Dave   But she (be) _____ only a tourist! She (ask) _____ me the way to Victoria Art Gallery, and I (tell) _____ her the way. She didn't (understand) _____ English very well, so I (go) _____ to the art gallery with her. She (be) _____ Japanese. She (be) _____ very nice.

Anne   But you (have) _____ a date with Jane on Saturday.

Dave   I know. That (be) _____ the problem. I (be) _____ late for the date. And then Jane (see) _____ us in Bridge Street.

Wortschatztraining

3. Was ist überzählig?

Welches Wort in jeder Zeile paßt nicht zu den übrigen?

1. tennis   swimming   gym   badminton   jogging
2. bridge   restaurant   pub   post office   library
3. went   ate   played   met   go
4. morning   tomorrow   afternoon   evening   night
5. where   when   white   what   who

4. Das Wort wählen

Wählen Sie aus jeder der obigen Gruppen ein Wort zur Ergänzung der Sätze.

1. Did you go to the pool yesterday?
   No, I don't really like _____.
2. I wanted some stamps, so I went to the _____.
3. I _____ Philip at the gym yesterday.
4. We all got up at 7.00 this _____.
5. _____ did she buy?

Grammatik im Visier

5. Plural

Bilden Sie die Pluralformen der Wörter in der Tabelle.

Singular	Plural
I	we
child	
man	
library	
church	

Singular	Plural
shoe	
woman	
family	
this	
person	

6. *was* oder *were*?

Setzen Sie *was* oder *were* in die Lücken ein.

1. These shoes _____ very expensive.
2. Her boss's name _____ John Brooks.
3. How _____ your weekend?
4. Where _____ Dave and Jane yesterday?
5. My son _____ ten on Tuesday.
6. Who _____ in the pub yesterday?

7. Fragen

Bilden Sie die passenden Fragen zu den Antworten, wie im Beispiel gezeigt.

Beispiel: What time *did you go to the pub?*
We went to the pub at 7.30.

1. Where _____?
   I went to London yesterday.
2. When _____?
   I met her on Sunday.
3. What _____ at the restaurant?
   He ate fish.
4. How many _____ from the library?
   I borrowed three books.
5. Where _____ shopping?
   They went shopping in Bristol.
6. What time _____ on Sunday?
   She got up at 10.00.

Leseecke

8. Janes Tagebuch

Jane schreibt immer Tagebuch, bevor sie zu Bett geht. Lesen Sie diesen Abschnitt und beantworten Sie die Fragen.

SATURDAY

I was really angry today. I had a date with Dave, and I was a bit late. Then I saw him in Bridge Street. With a woman. I didn't know her. She was very pretty. She saw me, and then David saw me. But he just looked at me. He didn't say anything. Who was she? Was she his new girlfriend? I was angry, so I went home. I called mum, and told her the story. She wasn't surprised. Then Dave called, and we had a big argument. I don't really like him any more. I told him - he was a bit surprised.

GOODBYE, DAVE!!!

Beispiel: Who did Jane have a date with?   She had a date with Dave.

1. Where did Jane see Dave?
2. Who was he with?
3. Did Dave and the woman see Jane?
4. Where did Jane go?
5. Who did Jane call?
6. Who called Jane?

Schreibprobe

9. What did they do?

Diese Leute haben alle Zettel geschrieben, um sich an ihre verschiedenen Wochenendverabredungen zu erinnern. Bilden Sie wie im Beispiel Fragen und Antworten darüber, was sie am Wochenende gemacht haben.

Beispiel: F: What did Liz do on Sunday morning?
A: She played tennis.

(6 SUNDAY a.m. - tennis) Liz

1. F:
   A:
2. F:
   A:
3. F:
   A:
4. F:
   A:
5. F:
   A:

Jane — evening: visit parents (4 Friday, 5 S...)

Dave — Sat 5 a.m. - meet Joe

Philip — 5 SAT p.m. - gym; 6 SUN

Anne — SUN 6 evening: drink with Maria

Sue — FRIDAY 4 evening - TV!

Lektion 9: *Wir sind zelten gefahren.*

In Lektion 9 geht es um Verkehrsmittel und Urlaub. Sie finden außerdem weitere Übungen zur Vergangenheit und lernen, wie man Jahreszahlen ausspricht.

Paare

1. Kurze Antworten

Ordnen Sie die Fragen den Antworten zu.

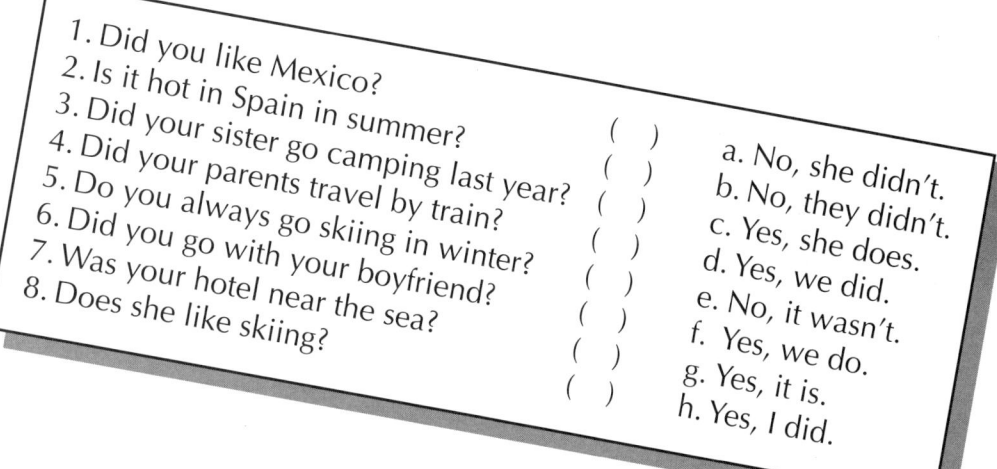

1. Did you like Mexico? ( )
2. Is it hot in Spain in summer? ( )
3. Did your sister go camping last year? ( )
4. Did your parents travel by train? ( )
5. Do you always go skiing in winter? ( )
6. Did you go with your boyfriend? ( )
7. Was your hotel near the sea? ( )
8. Does she like skiing? ( )

a. No, she didn't.
b. No, they didn't.
c. Yes, she does.
d. Yes, we did.
e. No, it wasn't.
f. Yes, we do.
g. Yes, it is.
h. Yes, I did.

Sprechprobe

2. *Hotel or tent?*

Dave hat sich Reisebroschüren angesehen und plant seinen Urlaub, während er darauf wartet, daß sein Freund Simon auf einen Drink in den Pub kommt. Setzen Sie die richtige Form des Verbs in die Lücken in Daves und Simons Unterhaltung.

Simon   What are those? Travel brochures?

Dave   Yes, for my summer holiday. Last year I (go) _____ to Turkey, and I really (enjoy) _____ it.

Simon   Where (stay) _____ ? In a hotel?

Dave   Yes, it (be) _____ a big hotel, near the beach, with a pool, and a really good restaurant, and a disco every night.

Simon   I (hate) _____ those big hotels!

Dave   Really? Why? It (be) _____ good fun - I (eat) _____ a lot of good food, I (drink) _____ a lot of good wine and beer, I (swim) _____ , I (dance) _____ , and I (meet) _____ a lot of very attractive women! Where did *you* go last year?

37

Simon	I didn't have a lot of money last year, so I (go) _____ camping with some friends. We (have) _____ a great time.
Dave	Camping? Yuk! Wasn't it cold and wet?
Simon	No, it (be) _____ ! The weather (be) _____ good, and we (go) _____ hiking, and swimming, and sightseeing.
Dave	(cook) _____ ?
Simon	Sometimes we (cook) _____ , and sometimes we (eat) _____ out - in pubs, or cheap restaurants. And we (meet) _____ a lot of attractive women, too.
Dave	I don't believe you!

Wortschatztraining

3. Jahre, Jahre

Schreiben Sie die Jahreszahlen wie im Beispiel aus.

Beispiel: 1979   *nineteen seventy-nine*

1. 1985 _____
2. 1960 _____
3. 1881 _____
4. 1994 _____
5. 1700 _____
6. 1979 _____
7. 1990 _____
8. 1912 _____

4. How did you go?

Ordnen Sie die folgenden Wörter, um verschiedene Transportmittel zu finden.

Beispiel: ubs   *bus*

1. liccbey _____
2. inart _____
3. arc _____
4. nepal _____
5. axit _____
6. troobmike _____
7. acoha _____
8. roshe _____

38

Grammatik im Visier

5. Verben der Vergangenheit

Setzen Sie die Präteritum- und Präsensformen der Verben ein.

Präsens	Präteritum
go	went
eat	
swim	
drink	
enjoy	
like	
stay	
want	

Präsens	Präteritum
have	had
	saw
	told
	danced
	met
	travelled
	drove
	did

6. Verneinung

Widersprechen Sie den Aussagen, wie im Beispiel gezeigt.

Beispiel: They went hiking. (skiing) *No, they didn't go hiking, they went skiing.*

1. She swam in the sea. (pool) _____
2. They drank beer every night. (wine) _____
3. Liz and her family stayed in a hotel. (tent) _____
4. We went to Austria in 1989. (1988) _____
5. They travelled by car. (train) _____
6. He checked the oil in the car. (water) _____

Leseecke

7. Alles über Liz Stones

Lesen Sie die Informationen über Liz Stones und bilden Sie Fragen, die zu den Antworten passen.

Liz Stones was born in Ireland in 1944. Her mother was a teacher and her father was an engineer. The family came to England in 1954 - Liz was ten. They lived in London.

Liz went to university in Manchester. She studied economics. She was a good student, and she enjoyed university. She also enjoyed travelling, and she went to Europe, Africa and India by bus and train.

After university, she moved to Bristol, and she met her husband Philip there. They got married in 1969.

1. _____ In nineteen forty-four.
2. _____ In nineteen fifty-four.
3. _____ In London.
4. _____ In Manchester.
5. _____ Economics
6. _____ In nineteen sixty-nine.

Schreibprobe

8. Checkliste

Liz und ihre Familie fahren dieses Wochenende zum Zelten, und Liz hat eine Liste mit Dingen geschrieben, die sie heute zu erledigen hat. Bilden Sie Fragen und Antworten darüber, was sie gemacht hat und was nicht.

Beispiel: check oil and water in car ✓

Did she check the oil and water in the car? Yes, she did.

1. call camp site ✓
2. buy food ✓
3. clean car ✗
4. go to bank ✗
5. clean hiking boots ✓
6. check tent ✓

Lektion 10: Möchten Sie nun bestellen?

Lektion 10 befaßt sich mit Essengehen und Restaurants. Sie finden Übungen dazu, wie man im Restaurant bestellt und Lebensmittel einkauft. Dazu: alles über Maße und Gewichte.

Paare

1. Im Restaurant

Ordnen Sie die Fragen den entsprechenden Antworten zu.

1. Would you like anything to drink?	( )	a. White, please.
2. Salad or vegetables?	( )	b. No, tea, please.
3. Do you want some coffee?	( )	c. Yes, I'd like a ham salad, please.
4. Red or white wine?	( )	d. No, I'm a vegetarian.
5. Are you ready to order?	( )	e. Salad.
6. Are you hungry?	( )	f. Yes, some red wine, please.
7. Do you like meat?	( )	g. Yes, I am.

Sprechprobe

2. What would you like?

Jane will immer noch nicht mit Dave reden, aber nach zwei Tagen lädt er sie für ein Gespräch zum Mittagessen ein. Bringen Sie die Unterhaltung in die richtige Reihenfolge.

1. **Jane**   Yes, okay, a chicken sandwich. And some coffee.
2. **Jane**   I had their tomato soup last week, and it was horrible.
3. **Jane**   I don't know. I'm not really hungry.
4. **Jane**   And I'd like a chicken sandwich.
5. **Dave**   Chips, please.
6. **Dave**   Oh. Well, how about a sandwich?
7. **Dave**   Yes, I'd like a cheese omelette, please.
8. **Dave**   How about some soup? The tomato soup is good here.
9. **Dave**   What do you want?

10. **Dave**   Yes, one coffee and one orange juice, please.
11. **Waiter**   With a salad, or with chips?
12. **Waiter**   Are you ready to order?
13. **Waiter**   One cheese omelette and chips, and one chicken sandwich. Would you like anything to drink?

Dave   *What do you want?*
Jane
Dave
Jane
Dave
Jane
Waiter

Wortschatztraining

3. Fruit, vegetables, or meat?

Ordnen Sie die folgenden Wörter der entsprechenden Kategorie zu.

chicken, lettuce, apple, lamb, banana, pear, beef, potato, ham, peas, lemon, beans, carrots, pork, onion, sausages, orange, steak, strawberry

FRUIT	VEGETABLES	MEAT

4. Shopping list

Sehen Sie sich die Einkaufsliste an und schreiben Sie die Artikel und die Mengen aus.

Beispiel: 3 lbs potatoes   three pounds of potatoes

½ lb tomatoes	1. _____	1 lt milk	4. _____
2 pts beer	2. _____	8 oz ham	5. _____
1 kg apples	3. _____	1 gal. oil	6. _____

Grammatik im Visier

5. Zählbar oder nichtzählbar?

Schreiben Sie *a* oder *an* vor die Artikel, die normalerweise zählbar sind, und *some* vor die, die gewöhnlich nicht zählbar sind.

1. _____ red wine
2. _____ glass of wine
3. _____ yogurt
4. _____ egg
5. _____ soup
6. _____ bread
7. _____ apple
8. _____ beef
9. _____ sausage
10. _____ fruit
11. _____ cheese
12. _____ cup of tea

6. *Some* oder *any*?

Füllen Sie die Lücken mit *some* oder *any*.

1. Excuse me, do you have _____ Italian wine?
2. We have _____ Spanish wine, but we don't have _____ Italian wine.
3. Do we have _____ eggs in the fridge?
4. I'm sorry, but there isn't _____ fruit.
5. I'd like _____ cheese and _____ French bread.
6. I want _____ apples, but I don't want _____ oranges.

Leseecke

7. *Liz's letter*

Liz schreibt ihrer Mutter einen Brief und erzählt ihr von der Auseinandersetzung, die sie gestern mit ihrem Mann Philip hatte. Bilden Sie Fragen mit den angegebenen Wörtern und geben Sie dann kurze Antworten.

Philip and I had an argument yesterday - about food. He eats and eats and eats! And he never does any exercise. He's really big - in fact, he's fat! He always eats eggs and sausages and toast for breakfast, and he usually has a hamburger or a pizza for lunch. I buy yogurt and fruit and milk for him - then I open the fridge, and there's beer, and more hamburgers, and more pizza! He likes tennis, and swimming, and football - but only on the television. And he's fifty next year! What do I do?

1. yesterday/who/an/had/argument?
   ----
2. Philip/exercise/any/does/do?
   ----
3. he/a lot/breakfast/eat/for/does?
   ----
4. beer/hamburgers/buys/and/who?
   ----
5. often/tennis/he/does/play?
   ----
6. fifty/is/he/when?

Schreibprobe

8. Breakfast and lunch

Bilden Sie Sätze darüber, was Dave, Jane, Philip und Liz zum Frühstück und zum Mittagessen essen.

	Breakfast	Lunch
Dave	egg, toast, coffee or tea	soup or omelette,
Jane	orange juice, yogurt, toast	sandwich
Philip	eggs, sausages, toast, coffee or tea	hamburger or pizza
Liz	toast, tea	apple, cheese

Beispiel: Dave usually has an egg, some toast, and some coffee or tea for breakfast. He usually has some soup or an omelette for lunch.

1. Jane ------------------------------------
2. Philip ------------------------------------
3. Liz   ------------------------------------

Lektion 11: Können Sie Französisch?

In dieser Lektion geht es um das, was man kann und was man nicht kann, sowie um Jobs. Außerdem gibt es Übungen dazu, wie man nach Gründen fragt und wie man etwas begründet.

Paare

1. Verben

Ordnen Sie jedes Verb einem geeigneten Ausdruck zu.

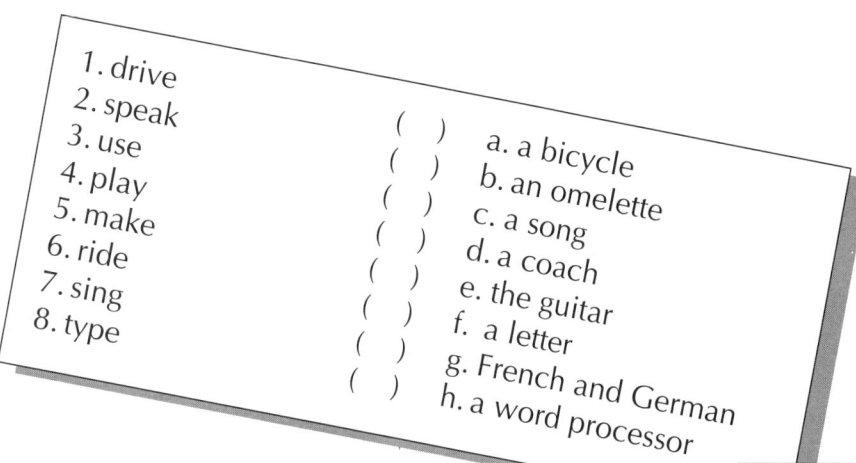

1. drive
2. speak
3. use
4. play
5. make
6. ride
7. sing
8. type

( ) a. a bicycle
( ) b. an omelette
( ) c. a song
( ) d. a coach
( ) e. the guitar
( ) f. a letter
( ) g. French and German
( ) h. a word processor

Sprechprobe

2. Yes, I can.

Jane will für eine Zeitlang aus Bristol weg – daher geht sie heute zu einem Vorstellungsgespräch bei einem Reiseveranstalter. Setzen Sie die geeigneten Verben aus dem Kasten ein.

Wortkasten: start, teach, use, speak (x2), love, drive (x4), type

Jane   I can _____ , and I can _____ a word processor.
Mrs Thomas   That's not important. We have lots of secretaries. Can you _____ any foreign languages?
Jane   Yes, I can _____ French and German, and a little Spanish.
Mrs Thomas   Good. Can you write them, too?
Jane   Yes, I can.
Mrs Thomas   And can you _____ ? Can you _____ a coach?
Jane   A coach! No, I can't. I can _____ a car, but I can't _____ a coach.
Mrs Thomas   Don't worry - we can _____ you. Do you like hot weather?
Jane   Yes. I was born in Australia - I _____ hot weather!
Mrs Thomas   Very good, very good. Would you like a job?
Jane   As a secretary?

Mrs Thomas No, as a tour guide. Would you like a job as a tour guide to Australia?
Jane Yes, I'd love it!
Mrs Thomas Good. And one more question - can you _____ tomorrow?

Wortschatztraining

3. Jobs

Ordnen Sie die Fragen den Antworten zu.

| cook   type   paint   drive   speak French   play the piano   sing |

1. Can you play the piano? — Yes, in fact I'm a pianist.
2. _____ — Yes, in fact I'm an artist.
3. _____ — Yes, in fact I'm a French teacher.
4. _____ — Yes, in fact I'm a secretary.
5. _____ — Yes, in fact I'm a chef.
6. _____ — Yes, in fact I'm a bus driver.
7. _____ — Yes, in fact I'm an opera singer.

4. More jobs

Wie viele Jobs können Sie im Wortquadrat entdecken?

```
L S M D O R P C E E D
O A E E S L O H P N O
F C P N U R S E A G C
F T I T V E T F I I T
P O L I C E M A N N O
E R O S O W A I T E R
L I T T P O N B E E E
L R E P O R T E R R S
```

46

Grammatik im Visier

5. Wh- Fragen

Beispiel: <u>What can Jane play?</u>   <u>Who can play the guitar?</u>
Jane can play the *guitar*.   *Jane* can play the guitar.

1. _____
You can see the doctor *on Tuesday*.

2. _____
I can see *Dave* from the window.

3. _____
You can buy some vegetables *at the supermarket*.

4. _____
You can cook *omelettes* for lunch.

5. _____
Liz and Philip can come to the party.

6. _____
Liz can sing *opera*.

6. Sätze mit *because* verbinden

Vervollständigen Sie die Sätze, indem Sie *because* hinzufügen und einen der im Kasten angegebenen Gründe wählen.

1. I'm sorry, I can't play tennis tomorrow because   <u>I'm busy</u>
2. I can't buy a new car because   _____
3. Dave couldn't come to the party because   _____
4. She didn't go swimming because   _____
5. I couldn't make an omelette because   _____
6. I can't go camping   _____
7. Jane couldn't eat her lunch because   _____
8. He didn't go to the library because   _____

```
a. He wasn't well.            e. I'm busy.
b. I haven't got a tent.      f. It was closed.
c. She wasn't hungry.         g. I didn't have any eggs.
d. I don't have any money.    h. It was cold.
```

Leseecke

7. Jane's note

Lesen Sie Janes Nachricht an Dave und beantworten Sie dann die Fragen unten. Beginnen Sie jeden Satz mit *because*.

1. Why can't she meet Dave for lunch tomorrow?
   _____

2. Why can't she see him next week?
   _____

3. Why didn't she tell him the news last night?
   _____

4. Why doesn't she like Bristol much any more?
   _____

5. Why does she like Australia? _____

> Sorry, but I can't meet you for lunch tomorrow - I've got a new job! In fact, I can't see you this week or next week at all - I'm really busy. I called you last night, but you weren't at home. Were you at the pub? Or with that foreign tourist. It's not important now. I don't really like Bristol any more - it's cold and wet. Next week - Australia! I love Australia - it's hot, hot, hot. So goodbye Bristol, and goodbye Dave.
>
> Jane

Schreibprobe

8. What can they do?

Bilden Sie Fragen und Antworten darüber, was Liz und Philip, James und Linda können und was nicht.

	play tennis	speak Spanish	ski
Liz	not very well	yes - a little	yes - a little
Philip	yes - very well	yes - very well	not very well
James	yes - very well	no	not at all
Linda	yes - a little	not at all	not at all

Beispiel: Liz/play tennis Can Liz play tennis? No, she can't play it very well.

1. Philip/speak Spanish _____
2. James/speak Spanish _____
3. Liz/ski _____
4. James and Linda/ski _____
5. James/tennis _____
6. Linda/speak Spanish _____

Lektion 12: Wiederholung

In Lektion 12 haben Sie die Gelegenheit, das in den Lektionen 1-12 Gelernte nochmals zu wiederholen und zu überprüfen.

1. Satzpaare

Ordnen Sie die Sätze einander zu, die eine ähnliche Bedeutung haben.

1. I'm married.	( ) a. Are you hungry?
2. I'm a vegetarian.	( ) b. We went to a restaurant yesterday evening.
3. I live in Bristol.	( ) c. Skiing is difficult.
4. Would you like something to eat?	( ) d. Did you speak to him yesterday evening?
5. Skiing isn't easy.	( ) e. They have a son and a daughter.
6. We all ate out last night.	( ) f. I'm not single.
7. They have two children.	( ) g. My home is in Bristol.
8. Did you call him last night?	( ) h. I don't eat meat.

2. A, B oder C?

Wählen Sie die richtige Antwort.

1. How do you do?
    a. I'm fine.
    b. How do you do?
    c. Thank you.

2. Would you like a drink?
    a. No, thank you.
    b. I'd like a drink, please.
    c. I like tea.

3. Are there any shops near your office?
    a. No, it isn't.
    b. Yes, there are.
    c. Yes, they're near.

4. Do you like your new boss?
    a. He likes me.
    b. I quite like it.
    c. She's okay.

5. How much is that blue shirt?
    a. No, it's a green shirt.
    b. It's fifteen pounds.
    c. There are three shirts.

6. Is the post office far from here?
    a. No, it's quite far.
    b. It's on the left.
    c. No, it's quite near.

3. Numbers

Schreiben Sie die folgenden Zahlen aus.

1. 1st _____
2. £4.50 _____
3. 16 _____
4. 60 _____

1. 10,500 _____
2. 3rd _____
3. 1984 _____
4. 75p _____

4. Gegensätze

Was ist jeweils das Gegenteil der angegebenen Wörter?

1. hot _____
2. always _____
3. bad _____
4. black _____
5. close _____
6. difficult _____
7. far _____
8. uncle _____
9. hello _____
10. single _____
11. men _____
12. summer _____

5. Fragen

Bilden Sie Fragen zu diesen Antworten.

1. _____
   They're 50p each.
2. _____
   I bought it yesterday.
3. _____
   It closes at 5.30.
4. _____
   Red.
5. _____
   She's 10.
6. _____
   Yes, I've got two sons and one daughter.

6. Vergangenheit

Wie lautet das Präteritum dieser Verben?

1. have _____
2. do _____
3. tell _____
4. speak _____
5. swim _____

6. come _____
7. go _____
8. meet _____
9. drink _____
10. drive _____

7. Verneinung

Verneinen Sie diese Sätze.

Beispiel: I wrote a letter to my mother. *I didn't write a letter to my mother.*

1. We went shopping yesterday. _____
2. The house has got a big garden. _____
3. He really likes his new job. _____
4. I bought some fruit this morning. _____
5. He gets up at 7.00 every morning. _____
6. They went camping last year. _____

8. Vermischte Sätze

Ordnen Sie die Wörter so, daß richtige Sätze entstehen.

1. size does what he ? shoes he take

   _____

2. is men's the the on floor second department

   _____

3. right our on house is second the

   _____

4. and family hotel a Liz in stayed her

   _____

5. cheese is fridge in there the any ?

_____

6. tennis because can't I'm I play busy

_____

9. Find the mistake

In jedem Satz kommt ein Fehler vor. Schreiben Sie die Sätze richtig um.

Beispiel: I went ~~their~~ last week.   I went there last week _____

1. The library is close on Sunday. _____

2. He hasn't got some children. _____

3. I usually have a soup for lunch. _____

4. We all went to London in train. _____

5. My sister and me went camping in France. _____

6. Excuse me, do you got any orange juice? _____

10. Kreuzworträtsel

Füllen Sie das Kreuzworträtsel mit Hilfe der Hinweise aus.

Waagrecht

1. How many days are there in a week?
5. A fruit, and a colour
8. Saturday and Sunday
10. A street
11. Men wear these.
12. Your mother's sister
13. You can drink beer here.
14. Make an omelette with these.
15. Small, green vegetables

Senkrecht:

2. Carrots and potatoes are these.
3. Opposite of yes.
4. You can drink this, or swim in it.
6. Is there a car in here?
7. Do you read this every day?
8. He works in a restaurant.
9. Evening meal.

Lektion 13: Wie sieht sie aus?

In dieser Lektion geht es darum, wie man Leute beschreibt und wie man etwas vergleicht.

Paare

1. Who's who?

Ordnen Sie die Wörter den Bildern zu.

1. tall
2. fat
3. dark
4. fair
5. strong
6. old
7. happy
8. slim

Sprechprobe

2. What does he look like?

Lesen Sie die Unterhaltung zwischen Liz und ihrem Mann Philip und sagen Sie dann, ob die Aussagen richtig oder falsch sind.

Philip I saw that new reporter of yours in the pub last night. He was rather drunk..

Liz Really? Who's that?

Philip I don't know his name. I saw him at your office party last week.

Liz What does he look like?

Philip Tall and slim. He's got long, dark hair. He's about 30.

Liz That's Dave Burton. He's got a big nose, but he's quite handsome. Is that him?

Philip Yes, that's him. He wasn't very happy last night. And he drank a lot, too.

Liz	That's because his girlfriend has got a new job – she went to Australia yesterday, as a tour guide.
Philip	That attractive young woman? With the short hair? She always wears big earrings?
Liz	Yes, that's right. Why? Do you know her?

1. Dave was at the pub last night.   True/False
2. Philip was at the office party last night.   True/False
3. Dave has got dark hair.   True/False
4. Dave is fat.   True/False
5. Dave drank a lot last night, because he was very happy.   True/False
6. Dave's girlfriend likes big earrings.   True/False

Wortschatztraining

3. Gegenteile

Wie lautet jeweils das Gegenteil dieser Wörter?

1. sad   _____
2. young   _____
3. cheap   _____
4. long   _____

5. fair   _____
6. tall   _____
7. big   _____
8. heavy   _____

4. Körperteile

Können Sie diese Körperteile benennen?

1. _____
2. _____
3. _____
4. _____
5. _____
6. _____
7. _____
8. _____

Grammatik im Visier

5. Komparative und Superlative

Setzen Sie die richtigen Formen der Wörter in der Tabelle ein.

Adjektiv	Komparativ	Superlativ
1. short		
2. old		
3. good		
4. long		
5. happy		
6. attractive		
7. heavy		
8. big		
9. easy		
10. slim		

6. Wortordnung

Bringen Sie die Wörter in die richtige Reihenfolge, damit Sie Sätze oder Fragen erhalten.

1. Mount Everest/world/mountain/the/the/is/in/highest

   ----

2. Liz/sister/beautiful/more/is/her/than

   ----

3. longer/Dave/he/hair/than/has/

   ----

4. world/longest/the/the/in/what/is/river

   ----

5. is/family/his/tallest/James/the/in

   ----

6. car/more/mine/expensive/was/your/than

Leseecke

7. Rendezvous mit einer Unbekannten

Daves Freund Joe hat ein Rendezvous für ihn mit Jenny arrangiert, eine von Joes Bekannten. In Daves Notiz an Jenny steht, wann und wo das Treffen stattfindet. Füllen Sie die Lücken mit Wörtern aus dem Kästchen.

> Hi – Can we meet on Friday? How about The Bell, at 7:30? I'm _____ Joe – but I'm _____ weight and height as _____ handsome! I'm also _____ than him. I have _____ black hair, and brown _____. I always _____ jeans and a black leather jacket. Sorry I _____ a photograph! See you on Friday.
>
> Dave Burton

eyes
haven't got
the same
long
wear
more
taller

Schreibprobe

8. Answer the questions.

Beantworten Sie die Fragen unten mit vollständigen Sätzen wie im Beispiel.

	Steve	Simon	Sue
Age	27	34	31
Height	189cm	184cm	178cm
Weight	74kg	92kg	61kg
Hair	dark, long	dark, short	fair, long

Beispiel: Who is the lightest?

Sue is the lightest.

1. Who is the heaviest?
2. Who is the oldest?
3. Who is the youngest?
4. Who is the tallest?
5. Who is younger than Sue?
6. Who is shorter than Steve?
7. Who has darker hair than Sue?
8. Who has the shortest hair?

Lektion 14: *Ich amüsier' mich ganz toll!*

Lektion 14 behandelt das Wetter. Außerdem finden Sie Übungen zur Gegenwart und zum Gebrauch von *so* bei Begründungen.

Paare

1. *The weather*

Ordnen Sie die Satzhälften einander zu und gebrauchen Sie dabei *so*.

1. It's snowing today	so… ( )	a.	we can't ride our bicycles.
2. It's raining today	so… ( )	b.	we can't see anything.
3. The sun is shining today	so… ( )	c.	I'm wearing my hat and gloves.
4. It's foggy today	so… ( )	d.	the children are all swimming in the sea.
5. It's windy today	so… ( )	e.	I'm sitting in the garden
6. It's very hot today	so… ( )	f.	I'm carrying an umbrella.

Sprechprobe

2. *Old friends*

In Sydney ruft Jane zwei alte Freunde an, Pete und Sally. Füllen Sie die Lücken in ihrer Unterhaltung mit einem Wort aus dem Kästchen.

Jane Hello, Pete? This is Jane, Jane Harris.

Pete Jane! How are you?!

Jane I'm fine. And you?

Pete Great. But where are you now? What are you _____ ? Are you _____ from England? Or are you here in Sydney?

Jane I'm in Sydney.

Pete On holiday?

Jane No, I've got a new job as a travel guide.

Pete You're _____ as a travel guide in Sydney! Great. Are you _____ in Sydney too?

> **visiting**
> **working (x2)**
> **cooking**
> **cleaning**
> **calling**
> **washing**
> **doing**
> **living**

Jane No, I'm not _____ in Sydney I'm just _____ Australia for ten days with a tour. How about you? What are you _____ ?

Pete At the moment? Right now I'm _____ clothes and _____ the house.

Jane Where's Sally?

Pete Sally's _____ at the office today. Hey, are you free tonight? Would you like some dinner?

Jane At your house? Who's _____ it?

Pete I am.

Jane Okay, I'd love dinner! What time?

Wortschatztraining

3. Was ist überzählig?

Machen Sie einen Kreis um das Wort, das fehl am Platz ist.

1. snow   hot   fog   rain   wind
2. working   skiing   swimming   hiking   skating
3. always   usually   sometimes   often   now
4. today   this morning   now   week   this evening
5. umbrella   gloves   hat   scarf   socks
6. newspaper   book   brochure   magazine   word processor

4. Welches Land?

Wo will Liz dieses Jahr ihren Urlaub verbringen? Für die richtige Antwort die Hinweise einsetzen.

1. Dave is ____ in a small flat in Bristol.
2. Jane is ____ a postcard to her parents.
3. It's hot today, so we're ____ lots of water.
4. Steve is ____ as a waiter.
5. The children are all ____ in the sea.
6. Liz is just ____ her teeth.
7. Who is ____ that song?
8. Philip is ____ in a chair by the pool.
9. They're ____ by train and bus.

Grammatik im Visier

5. Einfache Gegenwart und *-ing*-Form

Setzen Sie die richtige Form des am Satzanfang angegebenen Verbs ein.

1. (have) I usually _____ a shower in the mornings, but this morning _____ a bath.
2. (wear) She usually _____ a dress or a suit to the office, but today _____ jeans.
3. (drive) Philip usually _____ the family car on holiday, but today Liz _____ it.
4. (travel) We usually _____ by train, but this summer _____ by coach.
5. (cook) Sally usually _____ dinner at the weekend, but today Pete _____ it.
6. (go) The children usually _____ swimming on Saturday mornings, but this morning _____ skating.

6. *So* oder *because*?

Schreiben Sie die Sätze um und verbinden Sie sie mit *so* oder *because*.

Beispiel: It was Liz's birthday. We all went out to a restaurant.

It was Liz's birthday, so we all went out to a restaurant.

1. We're camping. We don't really like staying in hotels.

   _____

2. Today is my birthday. I'm having a party.

   _____

3. I'm staying at home today. It's raining.

   _____

4. I couldn't go on holiday last year. I didn't have any money.

   _____

5. The children are all sleeping. It's very quiet.

   _____

6. I love skiing. I always go to Austria or Switzerland for my holiday.

   _____

Leseecke

7. Jane's postcard

Jane hat folgende Postkarte geschrieben. Bilden Sie Fragen dazu, die zu den Antworten unten passen.

Beispiel: **Where is she sitting?** — By the pool.

1. _____ A cold beer.
2. _____ Thirty-five.
3. _____ Yesterday.
4. _____ Three.
5. _____ No, he isn't.

> Dear Mum and Dad,
>
> I'm having a great time. The sun is shining, I'm sitting by the hotel pool, and I'm drinking a very cold beer! But today is my only free day. There are 35 people in the tour group, and there's only one tour guide – me! – so I'm usually very busy. Yesterday I phoned my old friends Pete and Sally – do you remember them? They're both well – and they've got three children now! Sally is working at a computer company, but Pete isn't working – he's at home taking care of the children.

Schreibprobe

8. He is, he isn't

Bilden Sie Sätze mit den Hinweisen, wie im Beispiel gezeigt.

Beispiel: **Jim and Linda aren't playing tennis, they're playing badminton.**

Jim & Linda	tennis	badminton
1. Liz	suit	dress
2. Jane	postcard	letter
3. Dave & his friend	wine	beer
4. James	as a waiter	as a postman
5. Linda	ski	skate
6. Dad	magazine	newspaper

Lektion 15: Hast du morgen etwas vor?

In Lektion 15 geht es um Einladungen, Plänemachen und Vorschläge sowie um die Monate.

Paare

1. Invitations

Ordnen Sie die Einladungen oder Bemerkungen auf der linken Seite einer passenden Antwort auf der rechten Seite zu.

1. Would you like to go to the theatre on Saturday evening?	( )	a. Yes, I'm playing tennis.
2. Are you free this evening?	( )	b. Great! What day is it?
3. How about watching that film on TV tonight?	( )	c. Never mind.
4. How about 7.30 in front of the station?	( )	d. I'd love to! What's on?
5. Are you doing anything on Sunday?	( )	e. Good idea.
6. I'd like to invite you to my birthday party.	( )	f. Fine. See you there.
7. Sorry, but I'm teaching all day on Tuesday.	( )	g. Why? What's happening?

Sprechprobe

2. Birthday invitation

Füllen Sie die Lücken mit den passenden Ausdrücken.

Kate Hello, Phil? This is Kate. Can I speak to Liz, please? Is she there?

Philip Hi, Kate. Yes, she is. (1) _____ – she's in the garden. (shouting) LIZ! KATE IS ON THE PHONE FOR YOU! She's just coming, Kate.

Kate Thanks. .....Liz, hi! (2) _____ . Are you busy?

Liz No, it's okay. I'm just doing some work in the garden. What is it?

Kate Well, are you free next Tuesday evening?

Liz (3) _____ .What's the date?

> Is that okay?
> We'd love to.
> By the way,
> I don't know.
> I think so.
> Never mind.
> Hold on a minute,
> Sorry to bother you.

Kate	The 2nd – June 2nd. It's John's birthday and some friends are going out to dinner at that new Indian restaurant. Would you and Phil like to come?
Liz	(4) _____ . Hold on a minute – I'm just checking my diary. Yes, I'm free. Oh, Phil is going to a meeting in Liverpool that day. (5) _____ I can come!
Kate	Good.
Liz	Where and when are we meeting?
Kate	At our house, about 6:30. (6) _____ .
Liz	Yes, fine. I'm looking forward to it. (7) _____ , what are you giving him for his birthday?
Kate	(8) _____ I'm thinking about a small camera, or maybe a watch.

Wortschatztraining

3. Die Monate

Schreiben Sie die Monatsnamen aus und fügen Sie die fehlenden drei hinzu. Numerieren Sie dann jeden Monat in der richtigen Reihenfolge – der erste Monat ist 1 usw.

1. ____ Mar. _____
2. ____ Nov. _____
3. ____ Apr. _____
4. ____ Jan. _____
5. ____ Dec. _____
6. ____ Aug. _____
7. ____ Feb _____
8. ____ Oct _____
9. ____ Sept _____
10. ____ _____
11. ____ _____
12. ____ _____

4. How about going to...

Unten sind einige Orte oder Ereignisse genannt, zu denen man Sie vielleicht einlädt. Ordnen Sie die Buchstaben, um herauszufinden, worum es sich handelt.

1. micean _____
2. heatter _____
3. unseattarr _____
4. talebl _____
5. tryap _____
6. docis _____
7. roccent _____
8. esummu _____

Grammatik im Visier

5. How about....?

Ändern Sie die Fragen in Vorschläge um, wie im Beispiel gezeigt.

Beispiel: Would you like to play tennis on Tuesday?
<u>How about playing tennis on Tuesday?</u>

1. Would you like to see a film on Wednesday?

2. Would you like to go for a walk this afternoon?

3. Would you like to play golf this Sunday?

4. Would you like to go camping in August?

5. Would you like to stay at home this evening?

6. Would you like to have a party on your birthday?

6. *Is/are* oder *do/does*?

Bilden Sie Fragen und gebrauchen Sie dabei *is/are* oder *do/does*.

Beispiel: What/you/usually/watch/TV? <u>What do you usually watch on TV?</u>
What/watch/TV/this evening? <u>What are you watching on TV this evening?</u>

1. When/Dave and Jenny/go/the cinema?
2. How long/Jane/stay/Australia?
3. What/you/usually/do/weekends?
4. Philip/always/clean/car/Sundays?
5. What/they/see/theatre/tonight?
6. Liz and Philip/speak/French?
7. Dave/go/Spain/June?
8. Phil/come/ballet/Tuesday?

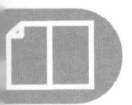

Leseecke

7. Das Grillfest

Janes Freunde Pete und Sally geben ein Grillfest für sie. Hier ist eine Einladung an einige ihrer Freunde. Bringen Sie die Zeilen in die richtige Reihenfolge.

> Dear Tom,
> 1. coming, and Julie and Ian are coming too – with their
> 2. afternoon? An old friend is visiting from
> 3. her. We've got lots of food and beer, so you just
> 4. seeing you here – from about 2.00.
> 5. bring the family, and your swimming things. The Thompsons are
> 6. Hi, how are you? Here's an invitation – would you
> 7. England, and we're having a barbecue for
> 8. like to come around to our house on Sunday
> 9. three dogs! We're looking forward to
>
> Pete and Sally

Schreibprobe

8. Tennisspiel

Zwei Freunde versuchen, ein Tennisspiel zu organisieren. Sehen Sie sich den Kalender an und antworten Sie wie im Beispiel auf die vorgeschlagenen Zeiten.

Beispiel: How about Monday evening?   I'm sorry, but I'm going to see a film with my family on Monday evening.

MAY						
Mon	Tue	Wed	Thur	Fri	Sat	Sun
3 6:30 to film with family	4 10:00-doctor 6:00 visit Mum	5 2:00: golf with Tom party at Liz's	6 Take care of children	7 paint the bathroom	8 9:30 take children to children's theatre	9 church tea at Mum's

1. How about Tuesday evening?   _____
2. How about the afternoon of the fifth?   _____
3. How about Thursday morning or afternoon?   _____
4. How about Friday 7th?   _____
5. How about Saturday morning?   _____
6. How about Sunday morning?   _____

Lektion 16: Kommen Sie oft hierher?

In dieser Lektion geht es um höfliche Konversation oder Smalltalk. Anhand der Übungen lernen Sie, wie man Erlaubnis erteilt und darum bittet und erklärt, wie oft man etwas macht.

Paare

1. *I was, too...*

Ordnen Sie die Aussagen auf der linken Seite einer Antwort auf der rechten Seite zu.

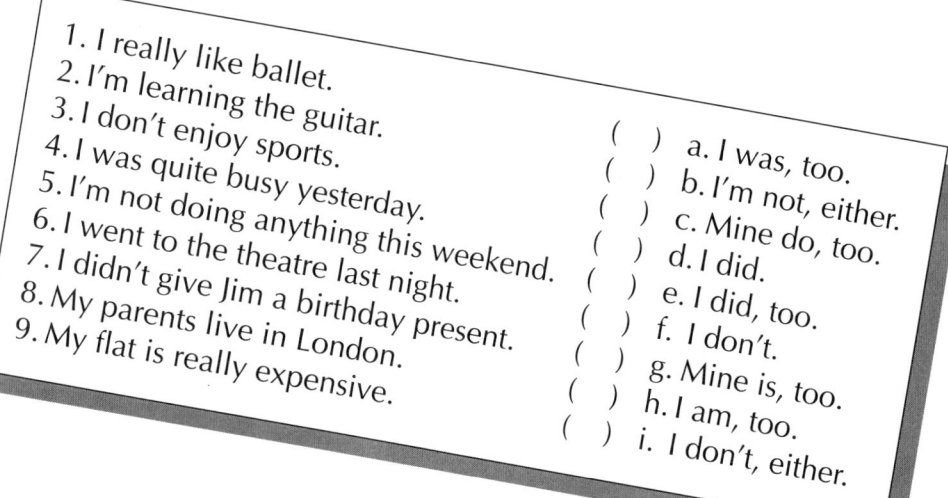

1. I really like ballet.
2. I'm learning the guitar.
3. I don't enjoy sports.
4. I was quite busy yesterday.
5. I'm not doing anything this weekend.
6. I went to the theatre last night.
7. I didn't give Jim a birthday present.
8. My parents live in London.
9. My flat is really expensive.

( ) a. I was, too.
( ) b. I'm not, either.
( ) c. Mine do, too.
( ) d. I did.
( ) e. I did, too.
( ) f. I don't.
( ) g. Mine is, too.
( ) h. I am, too.
( ) i. I don't, either.

Sprechprobe

2. Smalltalk

Füllen Sie die Lücken mit *a, the* oder einem »x«, wenn kein Artikel notwendig ist.

Jenny This is _____ nice pub, isn't it? Do you come here often?

Dave Yes – two or three times _____ week. How about you? What do you like doing in your free time?

Jenny Let's see. I like _____ singing, and I'm learning _____ guitar. I have _____ lessons every Tuesday and Saturday. And I like _____ painting. And I go to _____ cinema quite often, too.

Dave Hey, you're quite busy, aren't you! Do you ever go to _____ theatre?

Jenny Yes, I love _____ theatre.

Dave I do, too. In fact, I've got two tickets for _____ Theatre Royal for _____ Friday evening – would you like to go?

Jenny Yes, thank you, I'd like that.

Dave Good. Let's have another drink. Oh, just _____ minute. Uh – do you mind if we go to _____ different pub?

Jenny No, I don't mind. But why? And who's that strange woman over there? What's she doing? Why is she looking at you?

Dave It's nothing. I don't know her. Come on. Let's go.

Wortschatztraining

3. Kategorien

Ordnen Sie diese Wörter den richtigen Kategorien zu.

a telephone, a football game, French, a calendar, a camera, TV, films, cooking, a computer, painting, plays, the guitar, a video, a clock, money, photography, typing

1. Things to learn _____
2. Things to watch _____
3. Things to see   _____

4. What is it?

Wählen Sie einen der Gegenstände aus den obigen Kategorien zur Ergänzung der Sätze.

1. _____ is a sport.
2. A _____ is a musical instrument.
3. _____ is a language.
4. A _____ takes photographs.
5. A _____ shows the date.

Grammatik im Visier

5. Bestätigungsfragen

Vervollständigen Sie diese Sätze, indem Sie eine Bestätigungsfrage anhängen, wie im Beispiel angegeben.

Beispiel: They're going out tonight, _aren't they?_ _____

1. You're Japanese, _____
2. You come here every week, _____
3. It's windy today, _____
4. They went to India last year, _____
5. You can play the guitar, _____
6. He comes to this pub often, _____
7. You don't like Dave, _____
8. That was a good party, _____

6. Asking permission

Bitten Sie jemanden um Erlaubnis. Beginnen Sie die Fragen mit *Do you mind if...?* wie im Beispiel.

Beispiel: You want to use somebody's telephone. *Do you mind if I use your telephone?*

1. You want to listen to the radio. _____
2. You want to call somebody at the office. _____
3. You want to read somebody's newspaper. _____
4. You want to borrow somebody's camera. _____
5. You want to sit next to somebody. _____
6. You're cold. The window is open. _____
7. It's hot. The door is closed. _____

7. Giving permission

Ordnen Sie die Antworten den Bitten zu und schreiben Sie sie an die richtige Stelle.

Beispiel: Do you mind if I use your telephone?
Of course not, go ahead. Who are you calling?

Give permission	Refuse permission
Of course not, go ahead. Who are you calling?	
a. No, of course not. It's rather cold, isn't it!	e. Yes, I do. Please only call me at home.
b. Not at all. Please sit down.	f. Well, there's no film in it.
c. No, of course I don't mind. What's on	g. I'm sorry – I'm reading it myself.
d. No, please go ahead.	

Leseecke

8. Wie oft ...?

Lesen Sie die Beschreibung, dann schreiben Sie die regelmäßigen Termine in den Kalender.

I'm quite busy, really. I have a part-time job as an English teacher, and I teach on Monday, Tuesday and Friday mornings. I go swimming every Tuesday and Friday evening, but I have a dancing class on the first Friday of every month, so I can't swim then. I go camping every year with some friends, and this year we're going to France, so we're taking French classes at the moment – we only study once a week, on Wednesday mornings, so we don't learn much. And I can't go next week because I'm going to the dentist (I see him once every six months). My mother comes to stay with me once a month, usually the first weekend, but this month I changed it to the second weekend, because I'm going to a party on Saturday evening.

Schreibprobe

9. Do you ever ...?

Beantworten Sie diese Fragen über Sie selbst.

Beispiel: Do you ever go camping?   *Yes, I go camping about twice a year.*
oder   *No, I never go camping.*

1. Do you ever go skiing?
2. Do you ever listen to opera?
3. Do you ever speak German?
4. Do you ever drink whisky?
5. Do you ever ride a bicycle?
6. Do you ever wear jeans?
7. Do you ever travel abroad?
8. Do you ever stay in a hotel?

Lektion 17: Ich werde viel zu tun haben.

In Lektion 17 finden Sie Übungen zum Futur. Sie lernen außerdem, wie man Ereignisse voraussagt und um weitere Informationen bittet.

Paare

1. Sätze bilden

Bilden Sie vollständige Sätze aus den Wörtern in den drei Spalten.

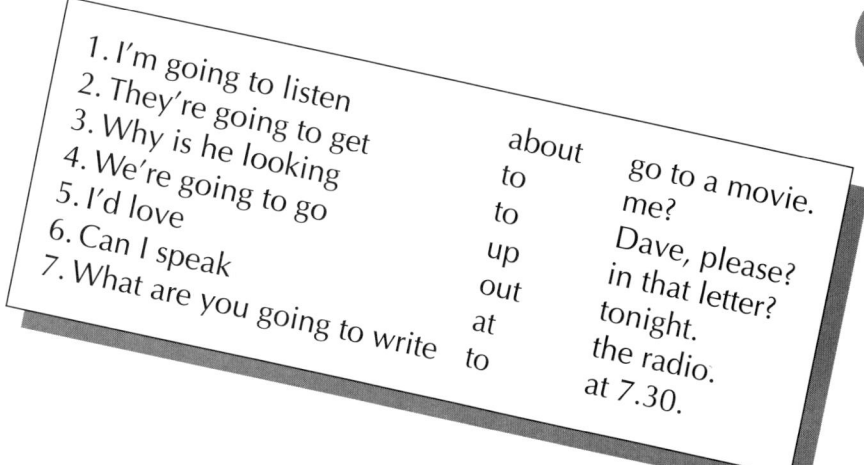

```
1. I'm going to listen
2. They're going to get        about    go to a movie.
3. Why is he looking           to       me?
4. We're going to go           to       Dave, please?
5. I'd love                    up       in that letter?
6. Can I speak                 out      tonight.
7. What are you going to write at       the radio.
                               to       at 7.30.
```

Sprechprobe

2. The argument

Liz hat eine Unterredung mit ihrem Sohn James. Finden Sie die richtige Zeilenordnung.

1. **James** No, I'm not going to pass, but it doesn't matter.
2. **James** I'm not going to get a job.
3. **James** No, not yet.
4. **James** I'm not going to university. I'm going to travel to India and then Australia.
5. **James** I'm not doing anything. Why?
6. **Liz** Not get a job? Well, what are you going to study at university?
7. **Liz** Why aren't you studying? Your exams are next month! What about your future!?Are you going to pass your exams?
8. **Liz** James, what are you doing in your room?
9. **Liz** Why doesn't it matter? What's going to happen after your exams? What job are you going to do?
10. **Liz** What?! And where are you going to get the money from? What are you going to do there? Why didn't you tell me? Did you tell your father?

Wortschatztraining

3. Das Verb wählen

Wählen Sie in jedem Satz das zutreffende Verb.

1. Be quiet – I'm *listening to/hearing* the news on the radio.
2. Are Liz and Phil going to *come/go* to our party?
3. When are you going to *speak/tell* your husband about this?
4. Did you *see/look at* that film on television last night? It was really good.
5. Do you mind if I *carry/bring* a friend to the concert?
6. I'm sorry, but I don't *understand/know* the question.

Grammatik im Visier

4. Klatsch – Fragen bilden

Antworten Sie auf diese Aussagen und gebrauchen Sie dabei wie im Beispiel *going to*.

Beispiel: We're going abroad this year.
(where/go) *Really? Where are you going to go?*

1. Dave is buying a new car this month.
(what kind) _____

2. We're painting the bathroom next week.
(what colour) _____

3. I'm taking Jenny to the theatre on Saturday night.
(what/see) _____

4. Pete and Sally are moving house next month.
(where) _____

5. Liz is having a small dinner party on Friday.
(who/invite) _____

6. Hey, I've got a new job!
(when/start) _____

5. *Somebody* oder *anybody*?

Ergänzen Sie die Sätze mit *somebody, something, somewhere, anything, anybody* und *anywhere*.

1. I'm not going to the party – there isn't going to be _____ interesting there.
2. Sshhh – I'm watching _____ interesting on the TV.
3. We haven't got much money, so we're not going to go _____ this year.
4. Is _____ coming for a drink?
5. Liz's office is _____ in Greenwood.
6. Dave is going to give me _____ really expensive for my birthday.
7. Liz? Are you there? _____ is on the phone for you.
8. I'm so hungry – is there _____ in the fridge?

Leseecke

6. Ihre Zukunft

Lesen Sie das Horoskop und verbessern Sie dann die Aussagen.

Your horoscope for this month.

Work:

This is not going to be a good month for you, so be careful! You're going to have some problems with colleagues at the beginning of the month, and money problems at the end of the month.

Love:

You're going to hear from an old friend – maybe a letter, maybe a telephone call, and this is going to cause problems with your partner – he's going to be jealous. There are going to be some arguments.

Health:

It's going to be a busy month socially – lots of parties and invitations, so take care of your health! You're going to need lots of exercise, sleep and a healthy diet.

Beispiel: You're going to have a good month for work.

No, I'm not. I'm going to have a bad month for work.

1. There are going to be problems with money at the beginning of the month.

2. There's going to be news from the family.

3. Your partner is going to be happy.

4. There are going to be arguments with your boss.

5. It's going to be a quiet month socially.

6. You're not going to need much exercise.

Schreibprobe

7. Linda's resolutions

Letztes Jahr hat Liz' Tochter Linda eine Liste mit guten Vorsätzen in ihr Tagebuch geschrieben, doch nun hat sie ihre Meinung über die meisten Sachen geändert. Schreiben Sie mit Hilfe der Angaben eine neue Liste für Linda.

Beispiel: marry ~~John~~ Steve

I'm not going to marry John, I'm going to marry Steve.

1. learn ~~guitar~~ piano
2. become ~~teacher~~ engineer
3. live ~~Canada~~ Brazil
4. drive ~~Rolls Royce~~ Porsche
5. be ~~beautiful~~ rich
6. have ~~dogs~~ horses

Lektion 18: Hin und zurück, bitte.

Hier geht es ums Reisen: Fahrkarten kaufen, Zugzeiten herausfinden, um die Wiederholung wichtiger Informationen bitten und höfliche Bitten äußern.

Paare

1. Gründe

Ordnen Sie jeder Frage eine passende Antwort zu.

1. Why are you going to London? ( )   a. To book a room for a friend.
2. Why are you going to the sports centre? ( )   b. To change some money.
3. Why are you going to the station? ( )   c. To see my parents.
4. Why are you going to the Station Hotel? ( )   d. To play badminton.
5. Why are you going to the bank? ( )   e. To get two tickets to London.

Sprechprobe

2. Buying train tickets

Jenny nimmt einen zögernden Dave mit nach London, um ihn ihren Eltern vorzustellen. Sie sind nun am Bahnhof und kaufen Fahrkarten. Vervollständigen Sie ihre Unterhaltung, indem Sie die Wörter aus dem Kästchen einsetzen.

Clerk Can I help you?
Jenny Yes, could I have two _____ to London, please?
Clerk Do you want day-returns? Are you _____ to Bristol today?
Jenny Yes, we are – two day-returns, please.
Clerk There you are. That's £68.80, please.
Jenny Sorry, _____ ?
Clerk £68.80. That _____ the underground.
Jenny Thanks. Could you tell me the _____ of the next train to London, please?
Clerk Let me see – the next London train is at 9.27, from _____ 3.

includes returning owe platform how much time returns stay

Jenny	Thank you. Come on, Dave.
Dave	But I want to _____ in Bristol today, and clean my car, and meet my friends, and go to the pub. Why are we going to London today?
Jenny	You know why – to meet my parents. Come on. And you _____ me £34.40.

Wortschatztraining

3. Wortpuzzle

Alle Hinweise sind übers Reisen und über Hotels. Setzen Sie sie ein, um ein weiteres Verkehrsmittel zu finden.

1. You can buy food on the train in the _____ car.
2. Do you want a return? No, a _____ please.
3. That's £35.00 for the room, _____ breakfast.
4. I'm going to the station to buy a _____
5. The London train goes from _____ 2.
6. I'd like a single room for two _____, please.
7. Can I pay by _____ card?
8. I'd like a _____ room for my wife and me.
9. One day- _____ to Birmingham, please.
10. Can you _____ travellers' cheques?
11. One single to London is eleven _____, please.

Grammatik im Visier

4. Informationen einholen

Stellen Sie sich vor, Sie können nicht verstehen oder hören, was jemand zu Ihnen sagt, und bitten Sie darum, daß man das eben Gesagte wiederholt.

Beispiel: The next flight to Tokyo is on *Wednesday*. I'm sorry – when?

1. The next coach to Bristol is *that blue one* over there. _____
2. Could I have two singles *to Birmingham*, please? _____
3. Mr Jones? You had a telephone call *from Mr Thomas*. _____

4. A single room is *£32.00* a night. ------------------------

5. The next train to London is from *platform 2*. ------------------------

6. I'd like *three* returns to London, please. ------------------------

7. The train arrives in Paris at *12.35*. ------------------------

8. The plane is going to be late, because of *fog in London*. ------------------------

5. Höfliche Bitten – *Could I …?*

Lesen Sie die Situationen und bilden Sie dann Sätze, die mit Could …? beginnen.

Beispiel: You want to know the time of the next coach to Bristol.

Could you tell me the time of the next coach to Bristol, please?

1. Somebody is speaking very quickly – you don't understand.

----

2. You want two return tickets to Liverpool.

----

3. You want to know the way to the station.

----

4. You are on a plane, and you want some water.

----

5. You want your taxi driver to stop just here.

----

6. You want to write something, but you don't have a pen – the person next to you has one.

Leseecke

6. *Jane's diary*

Jane schreibt kurze Notizen über jeden Ort der Reise in ihr Tagebuch. Lesen Sie die Notizen durch und bilden Sie daraus ganze Sätze.

Beispiel: Stayed in terrible hotel last night.

We stayed in a terrible hotel last night.

Stayed in terrible hotel last night. (1) Everyone in tour group very angry. (2) No double or twin rooms, and no showers! (3) Rooms dirty, and food in restaurant not good. (4) Wanted to find different hotel but too late. (5) Had argument with hotel manager – not a very nice man. (6) But all back to England tomorrow! (7) Flight arrives Heathrow 2.30 afternoon.

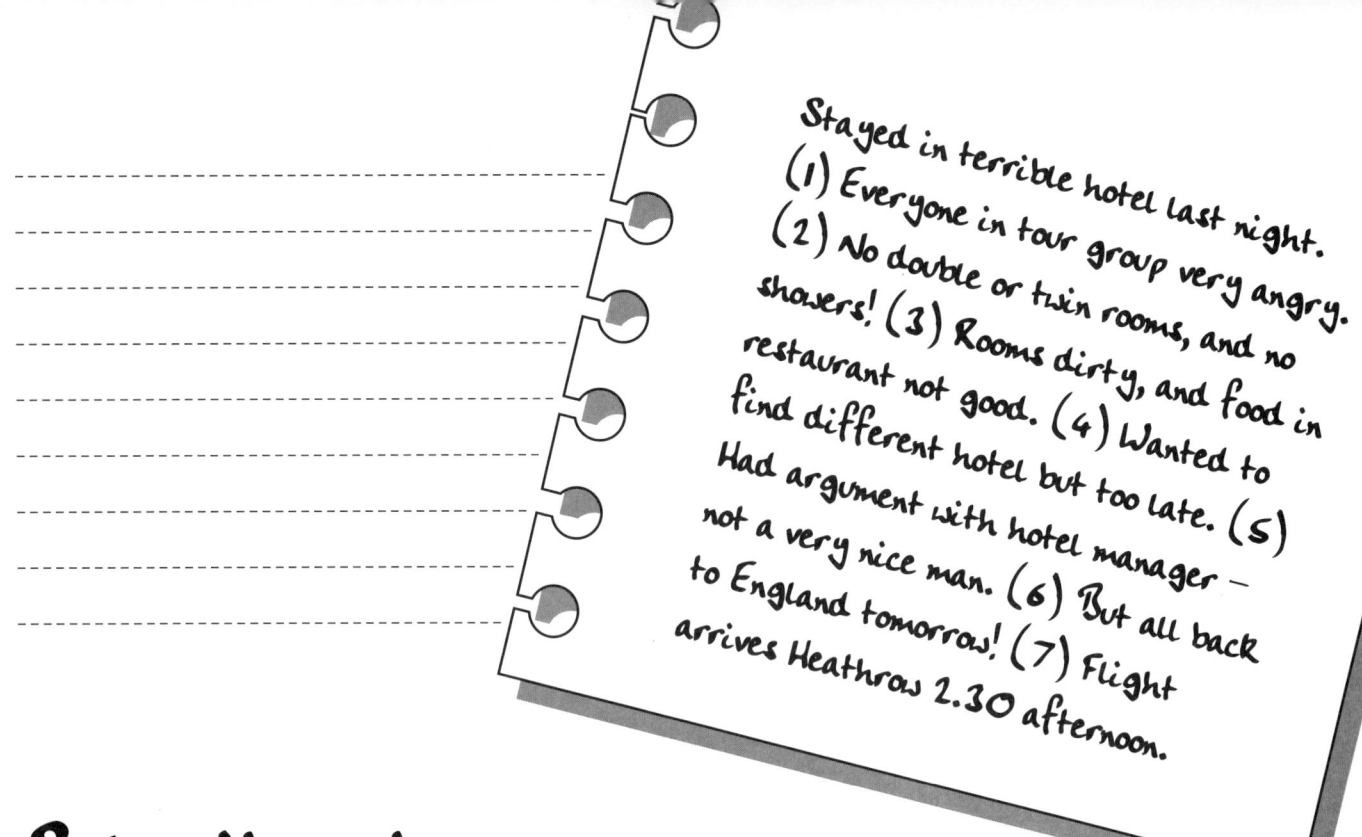

Schreibprobe

7. Could you tell me ...?

Schreiben Sie Unterhaltungen über den Fahrplan, wie im Beispiel angegeben.

Bristol	Bath	Didcot	London Paddington
06.04	06.19	06.30	07.50
(1) 06.57	07.12	07.23	08.45
07.42	07.57	08.08	09.20
(2) 08.12	08.27	08.38	09.52
10.12	10.27	10.38	12.00

Bespiel:

Passenger: Could you tell me the time of the next train from Bath to London, please?

Station clerk: Yes, it leaves at six nineteen.

Passenger: And how long does it take?

Station clerk: It takes one hour and thirty-one minutes.

1. Passenger: _____
Station Clerk: _____
Passenger: _____
Station Clerk: _____
2. Passenger: _____
Station Clerk: _____
Passenger: _____
Station Clerk: _____

Lektion 19: *Mir geht's schrecklich!*

Lektion 19 behandelt Gesundheit und sportliche Betätigung. Anhand der Übungen lernen Sie, auszudrücken, wie Sie sich fühlen, wie Sie Ratschläge geben und Körperteile benennen.

Paare

1. What do you do when you feel cold?

Ordnen Sie die Satzhälften einander zu.

1. When I feel cold ( )
2. When I feel lonely, ( )
3. When I feel tired, ( )
4. When I feel hungry, ( )
5. When I feel overweight, ( )
6. When I feel thirsty, ( )

a. I go to bed early.
b. I go to the sports centre.
c. I always drink water or juice.
d. I put on an extra sweater.
e. I make a cheese sandwich.
f. I call my best friend.

Sprechprobe

2. You look tired.

Jane ist gestern aus Australien zurückgekommen und trifft heute beim Einkaufen zufällig Dave. Vervollständigen Sie ihre Unterhaltung, indem Sie eine geeignete Verbform für die Lücken auswählen. (+) bezeichnet ein positives Verb, (–) ein negatives.

Dave Jane! Welcome back! How (be+) _____ the trip? You (look+) _____ rather tired.

Jane Yes, I am. We (have+) _____ a wonderful time, but it's a long trip back from Australia. I'm a bit jet-lagged. By the way, you look terrible! What (happen+) _____ ?

Dave I feel terrible. I have a headache, my stomach (hurt+) _____ , and I (can-) _____ sleep last night.

Jane Is it a hangover? Or have you got flu? Why don't you go home and go to bed?

Dave I can't – I (meet+) _____ someone in the pub at 7.30.

Jane A woman?

Dave Yes. In fact, I think she's the problem. Yesterday she (take+) _____ me to London, and I met her parents. We (have+) _____ lunch there, but her mother is a terrible cook. The food was awful, and I (be+) _____ sick on the train back. It was a horrible day. I (want-) _____ to see her any more.

Wortschatztraining

3. Körperteile

Ordnen Sie die Buchstaben so um, daß Sie die Namen für Körperteile finden. Markieren Sie sie auf dem Bild.

1. mathocs   _____
2. edah   _____
3. swirt   _____
4. gle   _____
5. dnah   _____
6. neke   _____
7. klean   _____
8. otof   _____
9. below   _____
10. dyob   _____

4. *Look* oder *look like*?

Streichen Sie das Wort *like* durch, wo es nicht nötig ist.

1. Jane LOOKS LIKE her father, doesn't she?
2. Paul is an accountant, but he doesn't LOOK LIKE one.
3. I LOOK LIKE so fat in this dress!
4. Liz LOOKED LIKE a bit ill yesterday – is she okay?
6. Is that your brother? You don't LOOK LIKE him at all.

Grammatik im Visier

5. Ratschläge

Geben Sie Ratschläge als Antwort auf diese Bemerkungen. Fangen Sie immer mit *Why don't you …?* an.

Beispiel: My eyes hurt. (wear your glasses)   *Why don't you wear your glasses?*

1. I've got a headache. (take aspirin)   _____
2. I've got horrible toothache. (go to dentist)   _____

3. I feel so cold. (put on sweater) _____
4. I feel terrible. (see doctor) _____
5. I feel so tired today. (go to bed early) _____
6. I've got a pain in my knee. (sit down) _____
7. I'm so overweight. (go on diet) _____
8. I'm so unfit. (get more exercise) _____

6. Verdrehte Sätze

Bringen Sie die Wörter in die richtige Reihenfolge, damit Sie Sätze erhalten.

1. bored/to/I/I/feel/the/go/when/pub/
   _____
2. see/why/doctor/a/you/don't/?
   _____
3. like/Dave/brother/look/doesn't/his
   _____
4. club/going/new/I'm/sports/to/that/join/
   _____
5. look/you/today/well/don't/very
   _____
6. headache/and/hurt/I/my/have/feet/a
   _____

Leseecke

7. Problemseite

Lesen Sie diesen Brief an eine Zeitschrift sowie die Antwort und korrigieren Sie die Aussagen, die folgen.

Dear Aunt Mary,

Can you help me? My problem is that I'm overweight. When I was a child, my mother made wonderful cakes and desserts, and I ate too much then! I was overweight when I was twelve years old! Last year I went on a diet, but I didn't lose any weight. I'm on another diet now, but it's just the same. And I can't sleep, because I'm always hungry. So I look terrible. And I'm so lonely. What can I do?

Patty

Beispiel: Patty's mother was a bad cook.

*No, she wasn't.
She was a good cook.*

> Dear Patty,
> When you are overweight, diet is very important, but exercise is important too. Do you do any exercise? Why don't you join a sports club, or an exercise class? You can meet lots of interesting people when you do sports. When you do exercise, you feel better, and you look better. Good luck.
>
> *Aunt Mary*

1. Patty didn't eat much when she was a child.

2. She lost a lot of weight when she went on a diet.

3. She looks terrible, because she's always hungry.

4. When you're overweight, diet and exercise aren't very important.

5. You meet lots of boring people when you do sports.

6. You look terrible when you do exercise.

Schreibprobe

8. When I was 12,...

Bilden Sie Sätze über die verschiedenen Ereignisse im Leben dieser Person. Beginnen Sie jeden Satz mit *When I …*

Beispiel: 12 years old, broke leg   *When I was 12 years old, I broke my leg*

1. Camping, Scotland, rained every day
2. University, wore glasses
3. Lived in London, jogging every day
4. Gardener, was really fit
5. Waiter, got really fat
6. Holiday, France, got flu

Lektion 20: Er schläft noch.

In Lektion 20 sprechen Sie über Ihre Erfahrungen und lernen, zu sagen, wie lange etwas gedauert hat.

Paare

1. Hasn't/haven't

Ordnen Sie die Sätze einander zu, die dieselbe Bedeutung haben.

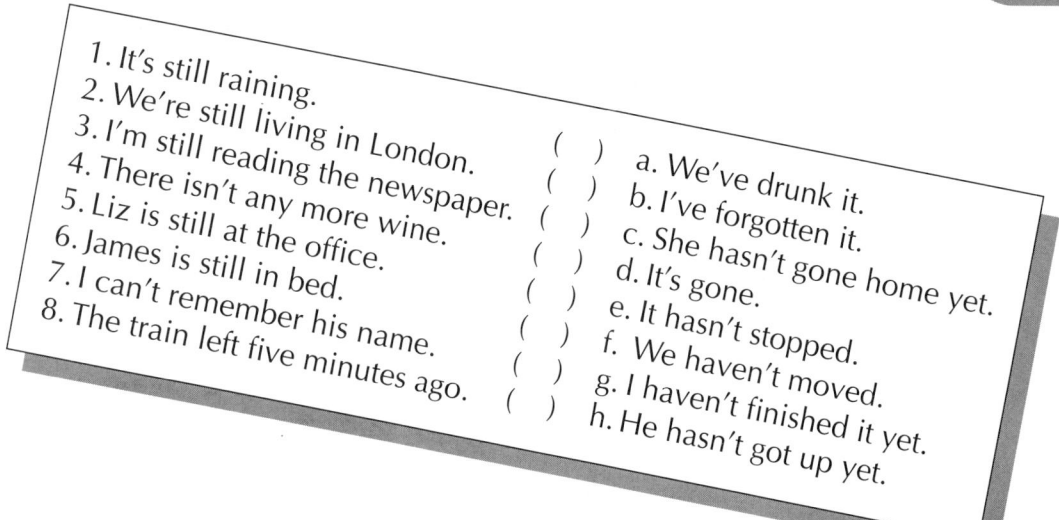

1. It's still raining.
2. We're still living in London.
3. I'm still reading the newspaper.
4. There isn't any more wine.
5. Liz is still at the office.
6. James is still in bed.
7. I can't remember his name.
8. The train left five minutes ago.

( ) a. We've drunk it.
( ) b. I've forgotten it.
( ) c. She hasn't gone home yet.
( ) d. It's gone.
( ) e. It hasn't stopped.
( ) f. We haven't moved.
( ) g. I haven't finished it yet.
( ) h. He hasn't got up yet.

Sprechprobe

2. He hasn't got up yet

Es ist Samstagmorgen, und Liz ist einkaufen gewesen. Als sie zurückkommt, sitzt ihre Tochter Linda in der Küche und trinkt Kaffee. Lesen Sie die Unterhaltung der beiden und sagen Sie dann, ob die Aussagen, die folgen, richtig oder falsch sind.

Liz Where's James?

Linda I don't know. I haven't seen him this morning.

Liz What? Hasn't he got up yet? It's nearly lunchtime!

Linda He went to the disco last night, didn't he? He's probably tired.

Liz I don't care. JAMES? JAMES! GET UP! IT'S LUNCHTIME! Linda, have you tidied your room?

Linda No, not yet. I'm going to do it this afternoon.

Liz But you're going to the jazz festival this afternoon.

Linda I know, I know.

Liz	Have you taken the dog out for a walk? You haven't, have you!
Linda	No, I haven't. Sorry, I forgot.
Liz	You forgot? Linda, what has happened to you? You forget so many things at the moment. Have there been any phone calls?
Linda	Yes, there were three calls, but they were all for me.

1. James is still in bed.   *True/False*

2. Linda saw James at a disco.   *True/False*

3. Linda hasn't tidied her room.   *True/False*

4. Linda hasn't taken the dog out.   *True/False*

5. They have eaten lunch.   *True/False*

6. There haven't been any phone calls for Liz this morning.   *True/False*

Wortschatztraining

3. *For* oder *since*?

Setzen Sie *for* oder *since* in die Lücken ein.

1. We've lived in New York _____ 1982.

2. Liz has been on a diet _____ her birthday.

3. Liz and Philip have been married _____ twenty-six years.

4. Dave looks terrible – he's had a cold _____ last Tuesday.

5. I've only known Dave _____ a month.

6. Pat has worked abroad _____ eighteen months.

7. It's been raining _____ 8.00 this morning.

8. Linda has been in the bathroom _____ an hour!

4. *Have you ever ...?*

Diese Sätze sind durcheinander geraten – schreiben Sie die Sätze richtig hin

1. Have you ever eaten your leg?   _____

2. Have you ever been to a golf?   _____

3. Have you ever ridden a department store?   _____

4. Have you ever played Australian wine?   _____

5. Have you ever lived in a horse? _____
6. Have you ever drunk Japanese food? _____
7. Have you ever broken your flat? _____
8. Have you ever worked in a pop festival? _____

Grammatik im Visier

5. Wortquadrat

Können Sie die Partizipien der folgenden Verben im Wortquadrat finden?

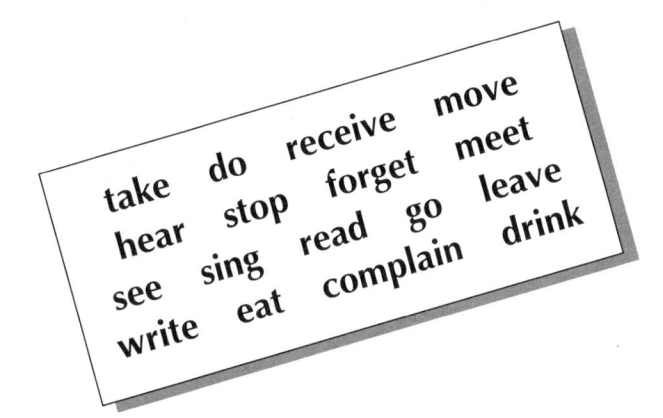

take do receive move
hear stop forget meet
see sing read go leave
write eat complain drink

```
S E L I T O O J R E A D
R A S U D D I H E A R D
O T L S S E E N C A C E
L E F T C C H N E L F T
O N C O M P L A I N E D
I S S P M N B O V L W O
P G A P R T A K E N R N
M O V E D G N A D J I E
H N D D R U N K C M T L
V E B O N N E C M E T O
Y E K F O R G O T T E N
E D I F T H A R S U N G
```

6. Die Zeitform wählen

Entscheiden Sie, welche Zeitform des jeweiligen Verbs in den Sätzen die richtige ist.

1. We went/have been to Switzerland three times.
2. Did you go/Have you been to to London by train yesterday?
3. I lived/have lived in Canada when I was a child.
4. How long are you/have you been married?
5. I met/have met Jenny's parents last Saturday.
6. James didn't clean/hasn't cleaned the car yet.
7. I'm sorry, but I forgot/have forgotten your wife's name. What is it?
8. The London train left/has left five minutes ago.

Leseecke

7. The jazz festival

Ergänzen Sie den Zeitungsartikel, indem Sie das entsprechende Verb in die Lücken setzen.

finish   complained   like   received   heard   lived   sleep   written

Complaints about festival

The police have _____ over a hundred complaints about the noise from the jazz festival in Greenwood Central Park last weekend. "I have _____ in this street next to the park for eighteen years, and I have never _____ such a terrible noise," said Mrs Pat Miller, of 24 Park Street. "It didn't _____ until 10.00, and our small children couldn't _____," said Mr John Taylor, of 37 Parkside Gardens. His wife, Mrs Jean Taylor, said, "We have _____ to the police, and we have _____ letters to the newspapers. We _____ jazz, but this music was horrible."

Schreibprobe

8. Have you done it yet?

Liz ist den ganzen Nachmittag nicht da, hat aber für James eine Liste mit verschiedenen Aufgaben hinterlassen. Sie ruft gerade an, um zu sehen, ob er sie erledigt hat oder nicht. Schauen Sie sich das Bild an und beantworten Sie Liz' Fragen mit Hilfe der Hinweise.

Beispiel: tidy/living room   Have you tidied your bedroom yet?

Yes, I've already tidied it. or *No, I haven't tidied it yet.*

1. clean/car

2. do/shopping

3. cut/grass

4. wash/ dishes

5. make/sandwiches

6. post/letters

Lektion 21: Na, wie gehts dir?

In dieser Lektion geht es darum, was man sagt, wenn man alte Freunde trifft, und wie man erklärt, was man gemacht hat. Außerdem lernen Sie, Ereignisse zu beschreiben.

Paare

1. So do I.

Ordnen Sie die Antworten den Aussagen zu.

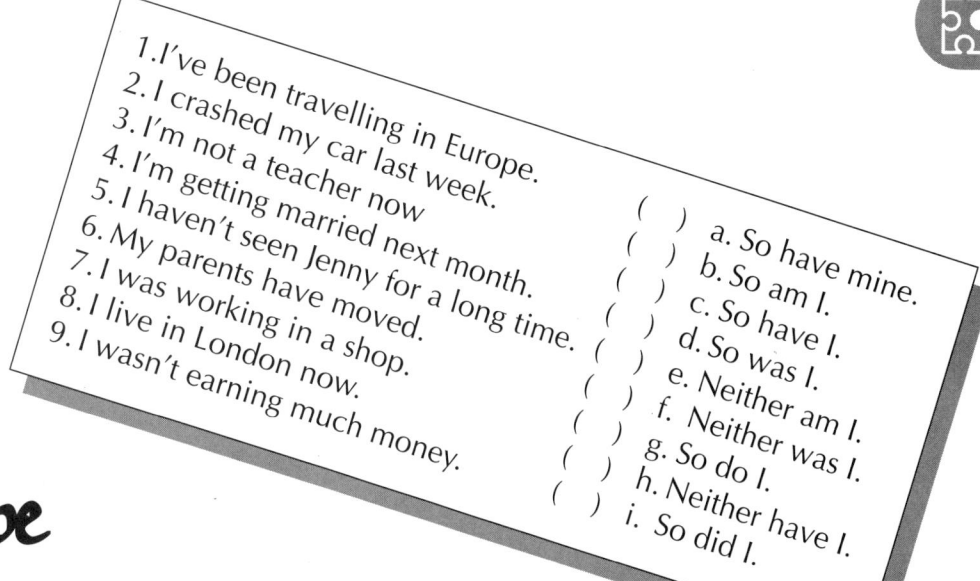

1. I've been travelling in Europe.
2. I crashed my car last week.
3. I'm not a teacher now
4. I'm getting married next month.
5. I haven't seen Jenny for a long time.
6. My parents have moved.
7. I was working in a shop.
8. I live in London now.
9. I wasn't earning much money.

( ) a. So have mine.
( ) b. So am I.
( ) c. So have I.
( ) d. So was I.
( ) e. Neither am I.
( ) f. Neither was I.
( ) g. So do I.
( ) h. Neither have I.
( ) i. So did I.

Sprechprobe

2. I haven't seen you for ages!

Setzen Sie die korrekte Verbform in die Lücken ein.

Jane Anne! I haven't (see) _____ you for ages! How are you?

Anne Jane, how nice to (see) _____ you. I'm fine. Hey, I (hear) _____ about your new job!

Jane Yes – I've been (work) _____ at the travel company for about two months now, and I really (like) _____ it. I haven't been in Bristol much, because I've been (travel) _____ in Australia. How about you? What have you been (do) _____ ?

Anne I'm still (work) _____ at the hospital. Hey, I (see) _____ your old boyfriend there yesterday.

Jane Who? Dave?

Anne Yes. I was (walk) _____ through the lobby, when I (see) _____ him.

Jane What was he (do) _____ there?

Anne I don't know. I was (talk) _____ to another patient at the time, so I couldn't (ask) _____ him. He was (sit) _____ in the corner, and he was (hold) _____ his head.

85

Jane	Oh dear. An accident?
Anne	Maybe. He was with a young woman. She (look) _____ very angry, and they weren't (talk) _____ .
Jane	Ah, a fight!

Wortschatztraining

3. Gegenteile

Was ist das Gegenteil dieser Verben?

1. lose _____
2. answer _____
3. buy _____
4. arrive _____
5. teach _____
6. receive _____
7. forget _____
8. wake up _____

4. Was ist überzählig?

Machen Sie einen Kreis um das Wort, das nicht in die jeweilige Gruppe gehört.

1. cupboard   newspaper   sofa   table   chair
2. walk   run   swim   jog   hear
3. customer   patient   horse   friend   boss
4. argument   talk   speak   tell   ask
5. bring   laughing   crying   working   finding

Grammatik im Visier

5. *Old friends*

Sie begegnen einer alten Freundin, die Sie jahrelang nicht gesehen haben. Stellen Sie Fragen zu den Aussagen Ihrer Freundin und beginnen Sie diese mit *How long...-ing?*

Beispiel: I make clothes now.   *Really? How long have you been making them?*

1. I'm studying Chinese now. _____
2. My sister lives in Brazil now. _____
3. My brother teaches economics now. _____

4. Pete buys and sells cars now. _____

5. My mother and father both play golf now. _____

6. I work at the hospital now. _____

6. When did it happen?

Beantworten Sie die Fragen, wie im Beispiel gezeigt.

Beispiel When did you meet your girlfriend? (work in London)
I met her when I was working in London.

1. When did you find the money? (clean the cupboard) _____
2. When did you break your arm? (ski in Austria) _____
3. When did they get married? (live in France) _____
4. When did Linda call? (talk to a customer) _____
5. When did he lose his wallet? (visit his parents) _____
6. When did you have the accident? (drive to Manchester) _____

Leseecke

7. Der Brief

Ordnen Sie die Zeilen um, damit Sie Janes Brief an ihre Mutter lesen können.

1. with his new girlfriend. They were having an argument, and his
2. time, and so I didn't buy your present - sorry. She's been
3. her yesterday! I was so surprised. I was shopping in
4. working at the hospital, and last week she saw Dave there
5. girlfriend was still hitting him there in the hospital! Ha ha ha!!
6. King Brothers Department Store for your birthday
7. Do you remember my old friend Anne? I met
8. weight, and she looks great! We were talking for a long
9. present, when I saw her. She's lost a lot of

Schreibprobe

8. What were they doing when mum came home?

Was passierte, als Mutti nach Hause kam? Schauen Sie sich kurz das Bild an, decken Sie es dann zu und beantworten Sie die Fragen unten.

1. What was the man reading? _____
2. What was the man eating? _____
3. Was he wearing a hat? _____
4. What was he sitting on? _____
5. Where were the children playing? _____
6. Was the girl laughing or crying? _____
7. What was the boy holding? _____
8. Where was the cat standing? _____
9. What was the cat doing? _____

Lektion 22: Was für eine Katastrophe!

In Lektion 22 üben Sie, das Futur mit *will* zu bilden, und über Wahrscheinlichkeiten zu sprechen.

Paare

1. Ähnliche Bedeutungen

Finden Sie ein Wort in der zweiten Gruppe, das in der Bedeutung einem Wort in der ersten Gruppe ähnelt. (Aber aufgepaßt – die zweite Gruppe enthält mehr Wörter, als Sie brauchen.)

> hate   okay   fat   go away
> probably   press   start   speak
> look at

> go in   find   also   see   begin
> weight   dislike   pull   tell
> maybe   right   overweight   talk
> push   leave   all right   finish
> horrible

Sprechprobe

2. Es wird nichts geschehen

Philip und Liz erwägen, am Wochenende wandern zu gehen. Lesen Sie ihre Unterhaltung und bilden Sie Fragen, die zu den Antworten unten passen.

Philip	I've been thinking about next weekend.
Liz	Yes? What about it?
Philip	Well, Friday and Monday are both holidays, aren't they?
Liz	Yes ...
Philip	Why don't we go away for a long weekend? Let's go to the mountains in Wales. We can go hiking.
Liz	But the children hate hiking.
Philip	We won't take the children. We'll leave them here.
Liz	What? Leave them alone?

Philip	It's okay, nothing will happen. They'll be all right. They can take care of themselves – they're sixteen and seventeen years old now.
Liz	I know, but .... What about food?
Philip	They'll probably eat hamburgers and pizza for breakfast, lunch and dinner. Don't worry about it.
Liz	They'll probably have a party, and drink too much beer, and ....
Philip	No, they won't. They're sensible children.
Liz	Well, I'd like to go away for the weekend ...... Okay, let's go.

Beispiel _What has Philip been thinking about?_ About the weekend

1. _____ He wants to go to Wales.
2. _____ No, they won't take them.
3. _____ No, they hate hiking.
4. _____ They're 16 and 17 years old.
5. _____ They'll probably eat hamburgers and pizza.
6. _____ No, they won't.

Wortschatztraining

3. Was wird passieren?

Ergänzen Sie die Sätze, indem Sie ein geeignetes Substantiv und Verb einsetzen.

> press (x2)   turn (x2)
> pull   lever   key   handle
> button   switch

1. What will happen if I _____ this _____ ? The window will go down.
2. What will happen if I _____ this _____ ? The lights will come on.
3. What will happen if I _____ this _____ ? The door will open.
4. What will happen if I _____ this _____ ? The engine will start.
5. What will happen if I _____ this _____ ? The radio will come on.

Grammatik im Visier

4. *If* oder *unless*?

Vervollständigen Sie die Sätze, indem Sie *if* oder *unless* in die Lücken einsetzen.

Beispiel: You'll be tired in the morning if you don't go to bed soon.

1. I won't speak to him again _____ he apologises.
2. You'll get fat _____ you don't do more exercise.
3. You're not having any lunch _____ you don't tidy your room.
4. She won't marry him _____ he loses some weight.
5. We'll miss the train _____ we don't hurry.
6. My wife will be really angry _____ I'm late tonight.
7. You won't pass your exams _____ you study hard.
8. No thanks – I'll get drunk _____ I have another beer.

5. *Myself...*

Setzen Sie *myself, yourself, himself, herself, ourselves, yourselves* oder *themselves* ein.

1. How did Philip learn French? I think he taught _____
2. Have you ever seen _____ on video?
3. Who's crying? Have the children hurt _____ ?
4. We had a wonderful holiday – we really enjoyed _____
5. Don't worry about me – I can take care of _____
6. Who's Jane talking to? She's talking to _____ !
7. Okay everybody, let's begin the party. Please enjoy _____ !

Leseecke

8. Partyeinladungen

Hier sind zwei Partyeinladungen, die durcheinander geraten sind. Können Sie sie aussortieren?

1. Mum and Dad are going away for
2. It's Jane's birthday next
3. weekend (she'll be 30!) so

4. the weekend, and they'll be away until Monday, so

5. we want to have a party for her. It'll be at

6. we're going to have a party! It'll be on

7. Saturday evening, from about 8.30. I'll probably

8. my flat on Friday evening, from about 8.00. I probably

9. cook food for the party, but could you bring

10. won't cook, because I won't have time, so could you bring

11. something to eat?

12. something to drink?

13. Thanks. See you Saturday – Linda.

14. Thanks. See you Friday – Sue.

Schreibprobe

8. Will you be all right if we go away for the weekend?

Liz stellt sich all die Dinge vor, die James und Liz anstellen werden, wenn sie und Philip fürs Wochenende wegfahren. Bilden Sie Sätze wie im Beispiel.

Beispiel: They'll probably have a party.

1. _____
2. _____
3. _____
4. _____
5. _____
6. _____

1. Get drunk? Yes!
2. Hamburgers for breakfast? Yes!
3. Tidy their room? No!
4. Take dog for a walk? No!
5. Sleep until 12.00? Yes!
6. TV all day? Yes!

Party? Yes!

Lektion 23: Was hast du gesagt?

In dieser Lektion werden Sie berichten, was Leute gesagt haben und wie sie es gesagt haben.

Paare

1. Wie hat sie es gesagt?

Ordnen Sie die Aussagen links einem entsprechenden Satzende rechts zu.

1. We're getting married!
2. My cat died yesterday,
3. James! Stop that!
4. That steak looks wonderful,
5. Ssshhh – the baby's sleeping,
6. It's 2.00 in the morning!
7. This is my tenth glass of wine,
8. That's his new girlfriend,

( ) a. she said hungrily.
( ) b. she said quietly.
( ) c. she said drunkenly.
( ) d. she said sleepily.
( ) e. she said angrily.
( ) f. she said jealously.
( ) g. she said happily.
( ) h. she said sadly.

Sprechprobe

2. What did he say?

Jane erzählt ihrer Freundin Anne von dem Anruf, den sie gestern abend von Dave erhielt. Schreiben Sie die Unterhaltung in Janes Worten um.

Dave	I'm calling to say goodbye.
Jane	Where are you going?
Dave	(1) I'm leaving Bristol, and going to London.
Jane	(2) Why are you leaving?
Dave	(3) There are too many problems for me here.
Jane	(4) What kind of problems do you have?
Dave	(5) I have all kinds of problems. (6) I don't like my job, my boss doesn't like me, and I'm having too many problems with girlfriends.
Jane	(7) What are you going to do in London?
Dave	(8) I don't know yet. By the way, (9) what are you doing on Friday night?
Jane	(10) I'm not doing anything. (11) Why?
Dave	(12) I have two tickets to the theatre.

Beispiel: He said he was calling to say goodbye.
I asked him where he was going.

1.
2.
3.
4.
5.
6.
7.
8.
9.
10.
11.
12.

Wortschatztraining

3. Adverben finden

Finden Sie heraus, wie Dave letzte Nacht nach Hause gekommen ist. Verwenden Sie die Hinweise, um das Wortpuzzle zu vervollständigen.

1. Do you play the piano well? No, I play it very _____ !
2. It's _____ hot today, isn't it!
3. I _____ go to the deli for lunch, but
4. 'I haven't eaten anything all day!' he said _____
5. We're late! Let's walk more _____
6. Children, you're too loud! Please play _____
7. Mum shouted at me really _____ when I broke her camera.
8. Liz plays tennis very _____
9. I'm sorry, that was too fast. Could you say it again _____

Grammatik im Visier

5. Adjektiv oder Adverb?

Machen Sie in jedem Satz einen Kreis um das Adjektiv oder Adverb.

1. Do you think Anne is jealous/jealously of me?
2. Your daughter plays the piano very good/well.
3. Could you speak a little more quiet/quietly please?
4. Dave was looking very unhappy/unhappily yesterday.
5. I walked quick/quickly to the station, but I still missed the train.
6. Be careful – the cat is looking very hungry/hungrily at your fish!
7. I'm sorry I shouted at you, but I was very angry/angrily.
8. I can't hear you because the television is so loud/loudly.

6. Yes or no?

Ändern Sie diese Sätze um, wie im Beispiel gezeigt.

Beispiel: 'Are you going home?' she asked him. **She asked him if he was going home.**

1. 'Is it cold outside?' he asked her. _____
2. 'Do you like films?' she asked him. _____
3. 'Do you want another beer?' Philip asked his friend. _____
4. 'Are you going abroad again soon?' Dave asked Jane. _____
5. 'Are your parents well?' he asked her. _____
6. 'Does your boyfriend play the guitar?' Jane asked Anne. _____

Leseecke

7. I heard it in the bank

Liz war auf der Bank, wo sie zufällig mit anhörte, wie zwei junge Leute hinter ihr eine sehr interessante Unterhaltung hatten. Als sie nach Hause kam, erzählte sie Philip davon. Lesen Sie, was Liz gesagt hat, und schreiben Sie dann die Unterhaltung in den Sprechblasen um.

'He asked her what she was doing this weekend, and she said she was going to a party. So he asked her where the party was, and she told him that it was in Greenwood, and that it was going to be a very good party. He asked her why it was going to be a good party, and she said because her friend's parents were going to be away for the weekend. So he asked her what her friend's name was, and she said her friend's name was Linda, and her friend's brother's name was James…'

Schreibprobe

8. What do you say?

Beantworten Sie die Fragen wie im Beispiel.

Beispiel: What do you say when you want to know the price of something?

You say, 'Excuse me, how much is this?'

1. What do you say when you want to know the way to the station?

2. What do you say before you go to bed at night?"

3. What do you say if you want to sit next to someone on the train?

4. What do you say when you want to know what time the library closes?

5. What do you say when you want to invite someone to a film tonight?

Lektion 24: Wiederholung

In dieser Lektion haben Sie die Gelegenheit, das in den vorhergehenden Lektionen Gelernte zu wiederholen.

1. Gegenteile

Was ist das Gegenteil von:

1. a little _____
2. clean _____
3. arrive _____
4. late _____
5. same _____

6. always _____
7. loud _____
8. badly _____
9. buy _____
10. find _____

2. Das Wort finden

Wie heißen diese Wörter?

1. _ _ rr _ _ _ _   Wear these on your ears.
2. _ _ rr _ _   The opposite of lend.
3. _ _ rr _ _   An orange vegetable.
4. _ _ rr _ _ _ _   Not nice at all.
5. _ _ rr _   Go quickly!
6. _ _ rr _ _ _   Not single.
7. _ _ rr _   You say this when you apologise.
8. _ _ _ _ rr _ _   Not today.
9. _ _ ff _ _   A hot drink.
10. _ _ ff _ _ _ _ _ Not the same.
11. _ _ ff _ _ _ _   Not easy.
12. _ _ gg _   You can't see well in this weather.
13. _ _ ii _ _   Do this in the snow.

3. is/are-do/does-have/has

Ergänzen Sie die Sätze mit *is/are, do/does* oder *have/has*.

1. _____ you mind if I don't eat all this?
2. How often _____ she call you?
3. _____ Dave got a new job in London?
4. _____ she going to have a party on her birthday?
5. What time _____ your parent arriving?
6. I _____ never been to Scotland.
7. When _____ you usually take your summer holiday?
8. Jane _____ just bought a new car.

4. Was klingt gleich?

Ordnen Sie die Wörter in Gruppen von drei, vier oder fünf Wörtern, die sich reimen.

fight height red die right said
late wake high why wear blue knew
break steak make night
head white straight chair weight bread do true care
late wait

5. Den Fehler finden

Streichen Sie in jedem Satz das Wort aus, das falsch ist, und schreiben Sie die richtigen Wörter hin.

1. James is the taller person in the family. _____
2. I think it's going to snowing tomorrow. _____
3. How about go to the theatre this weekend? _____
4. It was Liz's birthday, because I bought her a present. _____
5. Would you like to go camping on August? _____
6. She's gone shopping, isn't she? _____
7. I'm not doing something tonight. _____
8. I've been working here since three years. _____

6. Kreuzworträtsel

Waagrecht

1. Can you play any ____ instruments?
4. I always ____ when I see this film – it's so funny!
6. Jane isn't here – she's ____ shopping.
7. We're going to ____ in a hotel this year – camping is too wet!
10. It's my birthday ____ Tuesday.
11. I think it's going ____ rain.
12. I'm going to ____ an engineer when I'm older.
13. Have you ever ____ Linda's brother?
14. Dave and Anne were ____ born in London.
17. I haven't eaten ____ today – I'm so hungry now!
18. James, have you ____ the grass yet?
19. I didn't go on holiday last year ____ I didn't have any money.
23. Let's have drink at the ____ tonight.
25. You look tired – why don't you go to bed ____ tonight?
26. It's always hot on my birthday, because it's in ____ .
27. It looks cold outside – I think it's going to ____ .
28. You ____ unhappy yesterday – were you okay?
29. I don't play tennis very well at all. In fact I play very ____ .

Senkrecht

1. We'll ____ the train if we don't run.
2. We moved to Birmingham three years ____ .
3. I don't have any friends in Bristol – I feel so ____ .
4. ____ 's go abroad this summer.
5. Ouch! My head ____ !
8. How ____ going to see a movie tonight.
9. I haven't had lunch ____ .
15. ____ you ever been to Canada?
16. Those shoes are horrible, but ____ are nice.
20. I ____ run fast when I was younger, but I can't now.
21. I enjoyed the job, but I didn't ____ much money.
22. Please hurry – you're walking too ____ .
23. If he ____ that lever, the door will open.
24. Good – eggs and ____ again for breakfast!

7. Has she done it yet?

Liz hat heute sehr viel zu tun, daher hat sie eine Liste mit Dingen geschrieben, die zu erledigen sind. Es ist nun Mittag. Was hat sie alles getan und was nicht? Bilden Sie Sätze, wie im Beispiel angegeben.

Beispiel: buy bread ✓ Has she bought bread yet? Yes, she has.
cut grass   Has she cut the grass yet? No, she hasn't.

1. call mum
2. clean bathroom ✓
3. tidy bedrooms ✓
4. post letters
5. go to library ✓
6. take dog out ✓

8. The postcard

Postkarten werden gewöhnlich in Kurzform geschrieben – schreiben Sie diese Karte in ganzen Sätzen.

> Tuesday.
> V. hot every day, but raining today. Hotel is great – small, quiet, but big swimming pool, two restaurants. Lots of interesting people. Been swimming every day. Shopping difficult – don't speak the language! But local people v. nice, and food wonderful. Home on Saturday – see you then!
> Phil and Sue

It's Tuesday today _____

9. Fragen über Sie

1. What are you wearing right now?
2. Do you look like your mother or your father?
3. How is the weather today?
4. Where did you go on holiday last year?
5. How often do you go to the dentist?
6. Have you ever been on a diet?
7. Where did you live when you were a child?
8. How long have you been studying English?

NACHSCHLAGETEIL

Antwortschlüssel

LEKTION 1

1. AM-I; IS-she, he, it, Mike; ARE-we, Mr and Mrs Thomas, Liz and I, they, you

2. isn't, it's, I'm, you, meet, are

3. Spain-Spanish; England-English, Germany-German; Scotland-Scottish; Italy-Italian; the United States-American; Canada-Canadian; Japan-Japanese; India-Indian; Australia-Australian

4. one, two, three, four, five, six, seven, eight, nine, ten

5. 1-His name's Dave Burton. 2-They're from France. 3-What's your name? 4-I'm Liz Stones. 5-We're American. 6-It's coffee. 7-She's my girlfriend. 8-Where's my tea?

6. 1-She isn't French. 2-They aren't from England. 3-It isn't coffee. 4-Her name isn't Jones. 5-I'm not single.

7. Dave Burton is English. He's from Bristol. His address is 28 River Street. He isn't married, he's single. He's 31. His girlfriend's name is Jane. She's from London. She's 29.

8. Freie Antworten.

LEKTION 2

1. 1-d 2-e 3-b 4-a 5-f 6-h 7-c

2. a, a, a, a, an, a, a, an, a, a, an, a, a, a

3. Jane is twenty-nine. Sue and Peter are thirty-two. Mary is fifty-nine. Tony is sixty-two. Alice is eighty-one.

4. M, F, M, F, F, M, M, F, M, F, F, M, M, F 1-John 2-sister 3-husband 4-Jenny 5-son 6-niece, nephew 7-mother, father 8-grandmother

5. 1-has got two 2-has got one 3-has got one 4-have got three 5-have got two 6-has got three

6. 1-Have you got a car? 2-Has John got a girlfriend? 3-Where are Mr and Mrs Thomas from? 4-What is your boss's name? 5-How old are Sue's children? 6-What is her husband's job?

7. 1-No, he hasn't. He's got a new job. 2-No, he isn't. He's a reporter now. 3-No, it isn't. It's a big company. 4-No, it hasn't. It's got six branches. 5. No, she isn't. She's a photographer.

8. Is your address 47 Elm Avenue? No, it isn't. It's 47 Oak Avenue. Are you married? Yes, I am. What's your husband's name? It's Philip. Is he an accountant? No, he isn't. He's a teacher. Is he from Paris? No, he isn't. He's Scottish.

LEKTION 3

1. 1-a 2-d 3-e 4-g 5-b 6-f 7-c

2. in, are, There, Have, doors, behind, two, near, behind

3. yellow, red, blue, orange, brown, pink, white, black, purple, green

4. 1-shop 2-toilet 3-lobby 4-egg 5-gym

5. 1-some 2-a 3-any 4-a 5-any 6-some 7-any 8-an

6. 1-Is there a shower in the bathroom? Yes, there is. 2-Is there a washing machine in the kitchen? No, there isn't. 3-Are there any eggs in the fridge? Yes, there are. 4-Are there any restaurants in Greenwood? Yes, there are. 5-Are there any women in your office? No, there aren't. 6-Is there a pink carpet in the living room? Yes, there is.

7. 1-swimming pool 2-gym 3-public telephones 4-coffee shop 5-book shop 6-travel office 7-shofas, chairs and coffee tables 8-toilets 9-French restaurant

8. 1-How many bedrooms are there? 2-Is there a washing machine? 3-What colour is the living room? 4-Where's the garage? 5-Are there any trees in the garden? 6-Where's the garden?

LEKTION 4

1. there-chair-where eight-hate-late white-quite-right we're-near-beer new-you-do

2. 1-James is still in bed. 2-James has got Philip's newspaper. 3-Philip is ready. 4-Philip likes bacon and sausages. 5. Linda doesn't like meat. 6-Linda is a vegetarian.

3. 1-It's seven o'clock. 2-It's half past three. 3-It's eleven o'clock. 4-It's half past six.

4. 1-At half past seven he's in the bath. 2-At half past eight he's in his car. 3-At nine o'clock he's in his office. 4-At one o'clock he's in the sandwich shop. 5-At half past six he's in the gym. 6-At half past eight he's in the pub.

5. 6-3-1-5-4-7-2

6. 1-it 2-them 3-her 4-him 5-me 6-it 7-us 8-it

7. 1-she is 2-she doesn't 3-you aren't 4-I do 5-I am 6-they don't

8. c-e-a-d-f-b-h-g

9. 1-Does Jenny like shopping? Yes, she does. She loves it. 2-Do Liz and Jenny like dancing? No, they don't. They hate it. 3-Does Jenny like badminton? No, she doesn't. She doesn't like it at all. 4-Does Pete like pubs? Yes, he does. He loves them. 5-Freie Antworten.

LEKTION 5

1. 2-e 3-a 4-f 5-h 6-b 7-g 8-d

2. play, play, learn, learn, read, cook, watch, visit, eat, meet, meet

3. a-read b-drive c-watch d-play e-have f-write

4. (Mögliche Antwort: get up, have a shower/bath, eat breakfast, go to work, start work, have lunch, finish work, cook dinner, read the newspaper, watch TV, go to bed

5. 1-I always play football on Saturdays. 2-Anne often visits her parents. 3-Dave usually drives his car to work. 4-I don't often drink red wine. 5-Liz sometimes goes to the gym on Fridays. 6-Linda never eats meat.

6. 1-Do, they do 2-Does, he doesn't 3-Do, I don't 4-Do, they do 5-Does, she doesn't 6-Do, I do

7. at, to, at, at, to, in, to, on, in, to, to

8. Freie Antworten.

LEKTION 6

1. 1-c 2f 3d 4h 5a 6g 7b 8e

2. 1-He likes blue, grey and black. 2-No, he doesn't. 3-It's £55.00. 4-She wants a cotton shirt. 5-No, she hasn't. 6-No, she doesn't.

3. 1-shirt 2-sweater 3-socks 4-skirt 5-tie 6-jeans 7-shoes 8-jacket 9-blouse 10-coat

4. 1-seven pounds 2-one (pound) forty-five 3-four (pounds) ninety-nine 4-six (pounds) fifty 5-fifteen pounds 6-forty-nine (pounds) ninety-nine 7-one hundred and twenty-five pounds 8-five hundred pounds

5. 1-are 2-do 3-do 4-don't 5-is 6-does 7-is 8-aren't

6. 1-How much is this watch? It's thirty-five pounds. 2-How much are these ties? They're nine (pounds) fifty. 3-How much is this skirt? It's twenty-four (pounds) ninety-nine. 4-How much are these apples? They're fifty pence. 5-How much is this umbrella? It's seven (pounds) fifty. 6-How much are these socks? They're two (pounds) fifty.

7. likes, hates, likes, like, goes, buys, comes, cooks, eat, eat, cook, go

8. 1-What size does she take? 2-How much is it? 3-What colour is it? 4-How much are they? 5-Can I help you? 6-Where are the ties?

LEKTION 7

1. 1-e 2-g 3-c 4-a 5-h 6-b 7-f 8-d

2. near, see, there, over, on, your, outside, or, me, where, who

3. 1-first 2-second 3-third 4-fourth 5-fifth 6-sixth 7-seventh 8-eighth 9-ninth 10-tenth

4. 1-library 2-post office 3-swimming pool 4-bank 5-supermarket 6-butcher's 7-restaurant 8-pub

5. 1-on 2-on 3-at 4-on 5-on 6-at 7-on 8-at

6. 1-Excuse me, is there a telephone box near here? 2-The men's clothes are on the fourth floor. 3-The pub closes at half past ten on Sundays. 4-Turn right by the big hotel. 5-The library is open from nine o'clock on weekdays. 6-My house isn't far from here.

7.

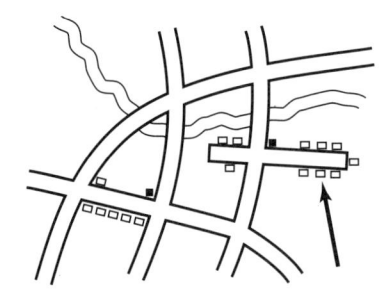

8. 1-When is the library open? It's open from ten o'clock to six o'clock on weekdays, and from ten o'clock to five o'clock on Saturdays. It's closed on Sundays. 2-When is the post office open? It's open from nine o'clock to half past five on weekdays, and from nine o'clock to half past twelve on Saturdays. It's closed on Sundays. 3-When is Casa Fina open? It's open from half past six to eleven o'clock on weekdays, and from half past six to half past eleven on Saturdays. It's closed on Tuesdays and Saturdays.

LEKTION 8

1. a-b 2-e 3-a 4-g 5-d 6-h 7-c 8-f

2. happened, had, have, saw, was, asked, told, understand, went, was, was, had, was, was, saw

3. 1-gym 2-bridge 3-go 4-tomorrow 5-white

4. 1-swimming 2-post office 3-met 4-morning 5-what

5. children, men, libraries, churches, shoes, women, families, these, people

6. 1-were 2-was 3-was 4-were 5-was 6-was

7. 1-did you go yesterday 2-did you meet her 3-did he eat 4-books did you borrow 5-did they go shopping 6-did she get up

8. 1-She saw him in Bridge Street. 2-He was with a woman. 3-Yes, they did. 4-She went home. 5-She called her mother. 6-Dave did.

9. 1-What did Jane do on Friday evening? She visited her parents. 2-What did Dave do on Saturday morning? He met Joe. 3-What did Philip do on Saturday afternoon? He went to the gym. 4-What did Anne do on Sunday evening? She went for a drink with Maria. 5-What did Sue do on Friday evening? She watched TV.

LEKTION 9

1. 1-d 2-g 3-a 4-b 5-f 6-h 7-e 8-c

2. went, enjoyed, did you stay, was, hate, was, ate, drank, swam, danced, met, went, had, wasn't, was, went, Did you cook, cooked, ate, met

3. 1-nineteen eighty-five 2-nineteen sixty 3-eighteen eighty-one 4-nineteen ninety-four 5-seventeen hundred 6-nineteen seventy-nine 7-nineteen ninety 8-nineteen twelve

4. 1-bicycle 2-train 3-car 4-plane 5-taxi 6-motorbike 7-coach 8-horse

5. ate, swam, drank, enjoyed, liked, stayed, wanted, see, tell, dance, meet, travel, drive, do

6. 1-No, she didn't swim in the sea every day, she swam in the pool every day. 2-No, they didn't drink beer every night, they drank wine every night. 3-No, they didn't stay in a hotel, they stayed in a tent. 4-No, we didn't go to Austria in 1989, we went to Austria in 1988. 5-No, they didn't travel by car, they travelled by train. 6-No, he didn't. He checked the water in the car.

7. 1-When was she born? 2-When did the family come to England? 3-Where did they live? 4-Where did she go to university? 5- What did she study? 6-When did she get married.

8. 1-Did she call the camp site? Yes, she did. 2-Did she buy the food? Yes, she did. 3-Did she clean the car? No, she didn't. 4-Did she go to the bank? No, she didn't. 5-Did she clean her hiking boots? Yes, she did. 6-Did she check the tent? Yes, she did.

LEKTION 10

1. 1-f 2-e 3-b 4-a 5-c 6-g 7-d

2. 9-3-8-2-6-1-12-7-11-5-4-13-10

3. Fruit: apple, banana, pear, lemon, orange, strawberry
Vegetables: lettuce, potato, peas, beans, carrots, onion
Meat: chicken, lamb, beef, ham, pork, sausages, steak

4. 1-half a pound of tomatoes 2-two pints of beer 3-one kilogram of apples 4-one litre of milk 5-eight ounces of ham 6-one gallon of oil

5. 1-some 2-a 3-some 4-an 5-some 6-some 7-an 8-some 9-a 10-some 11-some 12-a

6. 1-any 2-some, any 3-any 4-any 5-some, some 6-some, any

7. 1-Who had an argument yesterday? Liz and Philip did. 2-Does Philip do any exercise? No, he doesn't. 3-Does he eat a lot for breakfast? Yes, he does. 4-Who buys beer and hamburgers? Philip does. 5-Does he often play tennis? No, he doesn't. When is he fifty? Next year.

8. 1-Jane usually has some orange juice, some yogurt and some toast for lunch. She usually has a sandwich for lunch. 2-Philip usually has some eggs, some sausages, some toast and some coffee or tea for breakfast. He usually has a hamburger or a pizza for lunch. 3-Liz usually has some toast and some tea for breakfast. She usually has an apple and some cheese for lunch.

LEKTION 11

1. 1-d 2-g 3-h 4-e 5-b 6-a 7-c 8-f

2. type, use, speak, speak, drive, drive, drive, drive, teach, love, start

3. 2-Can you paint? 3-Can you speak French? 4-Can you type? 5-Can you cook? 6-Can you drive? 7-Can you sing?

4. ACROSS: nurse, vet, policeman, waiter, reporter DOWN: actor, pilot, dentist, postman, chef, painter, engineer, doctor

5. 1-When can I see the doctor? 2-Who can you see from the window? 3-Where can I buy some vegetables? 4-What can I cook for lunch? 5-Who can come to the party? 6-What can Liz sing?

6. 2-d 3-a 4-h 5-g 6-b 7-c 8-f

7. 1-Because she's got a new job. 2-Because she's really busy. 3-Because he wasn't at home. 4-Because it's cold and wet. 5-Because it's hot.

8. 1-Can Philip speak Spanish? Yes, he can speak it very well. 2-Can James speak Spanish? No, he can't. 3-Can Liz ski? Yes, she can ski a little. 4-Can James and Linda ski? No, they can't ski at all. 5-Can James play tennis? Yes, he can play it very well. 6-Can Linda speak Spanish? No, she can't speak it at all.

LEKTION 12

1. 1-f 2-h 3-g 4-a 5-c 6-b 7-e 8-d

2. 1-b 2-a 3-b 4-c 5-b 6-c

3. 1-first 2-four (pounds) fifty 3-sixteen 4-sixty 5-ten thousand, five hundred 6-third 7-nineteen eighty-four 8-seventy-five pence

4. 1-cold 2-never 3-good 4-white 5-open 6-easy 7-near 8-aunt 9-goodbye 10-married 11-women 12-winter

5. 1-How much are they (each)? 2-When did you buy it? 3-When/What time does it close? 4-What colour is it? 5-How old is she? 6-Do you have/Have you got any children?

6. 1-had 2-did 3-told 4-spoke 5-swam 6-came 7-went 8-met 9-drank 10-drove

7. 1-We didn't go shopping yesterday. 2-The house hasn't got a bit garden. 3-He doesn't really like his new job. 4-I didn't buy any fruit this morning. 5-He doesn't get up at 7.00 every morning. 6-They didn't go camping last year.

8. 1-What size shoes does he take? 2-The men's department is on the second floor. 3-Our house is second on the right. 4- Liz and her family stayed in a hotel. 5-Is there any cheese in the fridge? 6-I can't play tennis because I'm busy.

9. 1-close = closed 2-some = any 3-a-some 4-in = by 5-me = I 6-do = have

10. ACROSS: 1-seven 5-orange 8-weekend 10-road 11-ties 12-aunt 13-pub 14-eggs 15-peas DOWN: 2-vegetables 3-no 4-water 6-garage 7-newspaper 8-waiter 9-dinner

LEKTION 13

1. 1-f 2-d 3-b 4-h 5-a 6-g 7-c 8-e

2. 1-True 2-False 3-True 4-False 5-False 6-True

3. 1-happy 2-old 3-expensive 4-short 5-dark 6-short 7-small 8-light

4. 1-nose 2-mouth 3-chin 4-hair 5-eye 6-ear 7-teeth 8-neck

5. 1-shorter, shortest 2-older, oldest 3-better, best 4-longer, longest 5-happier, happiest 6-more attractive, most attractive, 7-heavier, heaviest 8-bigger, biggest 9-easier, easiest 10-slimmer, slimmest

6. 1-Mount Everest is the highest mountain in the world. 2-Liz is more beautiful than her sister. 3-He has longer hair than Dave. 4-What is the longest river in the world? 5-James is the tallest in his family. 6-Was your car more expensive than mine?

7. the same, more, taller, long, eyes, wear, haven't got

8. 1-Simon is the heaviest. 2-Simon is the oldest. 3-Steve is the youngest. 4-Steve is the tallest. 5-Steve is younger than Sue. 6-Simon and Sue are shorter than Steve. 7-Steve and Simon have darker hair than Sue. 8-Simon has the shortest hair.

LEKTION 14

1. 1-c 2-f 3-e 4-b 5-a 6-d

2. doing, calling, working, living, living, visiting, doing, washing, cleaning, working, cooking

3. 1-hot 2-working 3-now 4-week 5-umbrella 6-word processor

4. 1-living 2-writing 3-drinking 4-working 5-swimming 6-cleaning 7-singing 8-sitting 9-travelling (INDONESIA)

5. 1-have, I'm having 2-wears, she's wearing 3-drives, is driving 4-travel, we're travelling 5-cooks, is cooking 6-go, they're going

6. 1-because 2-so 3-because 4-because 5-so 6-so

7. 1-What is she drinking? 2-How many people are in the tour group? 3-When did she phone Pete and Sally? 4-How many children have they got? 7-Is Pete working?

8. 1-Liz isn't wearing a suit, she's wearing a dress. 2-Jane isn't writing a postcard, she's writing a letter. 3-Dave and his friend aren't drinking wine, they're drinking beer. 4-James isn't working as a waiter, he's working as a postman. 5-Linda isn't skiing, she's skating. 6-Dad isn't reading a magazine, he's reading a newspaper.

LEKTION 15

1. 1-d 2-g 3-e 4-f 5-a 6-b 7-c

2. 1-Hold on a minute 2-Sorry to bother you, 3-I think so. 4-We'd love to. 5-never mind. 6-Is that okay? 7-By the way, 8-I don't know.

3. 1-3, March 2-11, November 3-4-April 4-1, January 5-12, December 6-8, August 7-2, February 8-10, October 9-9, September 10-5, May; 6, June; 7, July

4. 1-cinema 2-theatre 3-restaurant 4-ballet 5-party 6-disco 7-concert 8-museum

5. 1-How about seeing a film on Wednesday? 2-How about going for a walk this afternoon? 3-How about playing golf on Sunday? 4-How about going camping this summer? 5-How about staying at home this evening? 6-How about having a party on your birthday?

6. 1-When are Dave and Jenny going to the cinema? 2-How long is Jane staying in Australia? 3-What do you usually do at the weekends? 4-Does Philip always clean the car on Sundays? 5-What are they going to see at the theatre tonight? 6-Do Liz and Philip speak French? 7-Is Dave going to Spain in June? 8-Is Phil coming to the ballet on Tuesday?

7. 6-8-2-7-3-5-1-9-4

8. 1-I'm sorry, but I'm visiting my mother on Tuesday evening. 2-I'm sorry, but I'm playing golf with Tom on the afternoon of the fifth. 3-I'm sorry, but I'm taking care of the children all day on Thursday. 4-I'm sorry, but I'm painting the bathroom on Friday. 5-I'm sorry, but I'm taking the children to the children's theatre on Saturday morning. 6-I'm sorry, but I'm going to church on Sunday morning.

LEKTION 16

1. 1-f 2-h 3-i 4-a 5-b 6-e 7-d 8-c 9-g

2. a, a, X, the, X, X, the, the, the, the, X, a, a

3. 1-French, cooking, painting, the guitar, photography, typing 2-a football game, TV, films, plays, a video, 3-a telephone, a calendar, a camera, a computer, a clock, money

4. 1-football 2-guitar 3-French 4-camera 5-calendar

5. 1-aren't you? 2-don't you? 3-isn't it? 4-didn't they? 5-can't you? 6-doesn't he? 7-do you? 8-wasn't it?

6. 1-Do you mind if I listen to the radio? 2-Do you mind if I call you at the office? 3-You do mind if I read your newspaper? 4-Do you mind if I borrow your camera? 5-Do you mind if I sit next to you? 6-Do you mind if I close the window? 7-Do you mind if I open the door?

7. 1-c 2-e 3-g 4-f 5-b 6-a 7-d

8.

June			June		
M₁	TEACHING		M₈	TEACHING	
T₂	TEACHING	SWIMMING	T₉	TEACHING	SWIMMING
W₃	FRENCH		W₁₀	FRENCH	
T₄			T₁₁		
F₅	TEACHING	DANCING	F₁₂	TEACHING	SWIMMING
S₆			S₁₃		
S₇			S₁₄		

9. Freie Antworten.

LEKTION 17

1. 1-I'm going to listen to the radio. 2-They're going to get up at 7.30. 3-Why is he looking at me? 4-We're going to go out tonight. 5-I'd love to go to a movie. 6-Can I speak to Dave, please? 7-What are you going to write about in that letter?

2. 8-5-7-1-9-2-6-4-10-3

3. 1-listening to 2-come 3-tell 4-see 5-bring 6-understand

4. 1-Really? What kind is he going to buy? 2-Really? What colour are you going to paint it? 3-Really? What are you going to see? 4-Really? Where are they going to move to? Really? Who is she going to invite? 5-Really? When are you going to start?

5. 1-anybody 2-something 3-anywhere 4-anybody 5-somewhere 6-something 7-somebody 8-anything

6. 1-No, there aren't. There are going to be problems with colleagues at the beginning of the month [or: There are going to be problems with money at the end of the month.] 2-No, there isn't. There's going to be news from an old friend. 3-No, he isn't. He's going to be jealous. 4-No, there aren't. There are going to be arguments with my partner. 5-No, it isn't. It's going to be a busy month socially. 6-Yes, I am. I'm going to need a lot of exercise.

7. 1-I'm not going to learn the guitar, I'm going to learn the piano. 2-I'm not going to become a teacher, I'm going to become an engineer. 3-I'm not going to live in Canada, I'm going to live in Brazil. 4-I'm not going to drive a Rolls Royce, I'm going to drive a Porsche. 5-I'm not going to be beautiful, I'm going to be rich. 6-I'm not going to have any dogs, I'm going to have some horses.

LEKTION 18

1. 1-c 2-d 3-e 4-a 5-b

2. returns, returning, how much, includes, time, platform, stay, owe

3. 1-buffet 2-single 3-including 4-ticket 5-platform 6-nights 7-credit 8-double 9-return 10-change 11-pounds [UNDERGROUND]

4. 1-I'm sorry - which one? 2-I'm sorry - to where? 3-I'm sorry - from who(m)? 4-I'm sorry - how much? 5-I'm sorry - which platform? 6-I'm sorry - how many? 7-I'm sorry - what time/when? 8-I'm sorry - why?

5. 1-Could you speak more slowly, please? 2-Could I have two returns to Liverpool, please? 3-Could you tell me the way to the station, please? 4-Could I have some water, please? 5-Could you stop just here, please? 6-Could I borrow your pen, please?

6. 1-Everyone in the/our tour group was very angry. 2-There weren't any double or twin rooms, and there weren't any showers. 3-The rooms were dirty, and the food in the restaurant wasn't good. 4-I/we wanted to find a different hotel, but it was too late. 5-I had an argument with the hotel manage - he's not a very nice man! 6-But we're all going back to England tomorrow. 7-Our flight arrives at Heathrow at 2.30 in the afternoon.

7. 1-Passenger: Could you tell me the time of the next train from Bristol to Didcot, please?
Station clerk: Yes, it leaves at six fifty-seven.
Passenger: And how long does it take?
Station clerk: It takes twenty-six minutes.
2-Passenger: Could you tell me the time of the next train from Bristol to London, please?
Station clerk: Yes, it leaves at eight twelve.
Passenger: And how long does it take?
Station clerk: It takes one hour and forty minutes.

LEKTION 19

1. 1-d 2-f 3-a 4-e 5-b 6-c

2. was, look, had, happened, hurts, couldn't, am meeting, took, had, was, don't want

3. 1-c-stomach 2-g-head 3-a-wrist 4-i-leg 5-f-hand 6-d-knee 7-e-ankle 8-j-foot 9-b-elbow 10-h-body

4. 1-looks like 2-look like 3-look 4-looked 5-looking 6-look like

5. 1-Why don't you take an aspirin? 2-Why don't you go to the dentist? 3-Why don't you put on a sweater? 4-Why don't you see a/the doctor? 5-Why don't you go to bed early? 6-Why don't you sit down? 7-Why don't you go on a diet? 8-Why don't you get more exercise?

6. 1-When I feel bored, I go to the pub./I go to the pub when I feel bored. 2-Why don't you see a doctor? 3-Dave doesn't look like his brother. 4-I'm going to join that new sports club. 5-You don't look very well today. 6-I have a headache, and my feet hurt./My feet hurt, and I have a headache.

7. 1-Yes, she did. She ate lots when she was a child. 2-No, she didn't. She didn't lose any weight when she went on a diet. 3-No, she doesn't. She looks terrible because she can't sleep. 4-Yes, they are. When you're overweight, diet and exercise are very important. 5-No, you don't. You meet lots of interesting people when you do sports. 6-No, you don't. You look better when you do exercise.

8. 1-When I went camping in Scotland, it rained every day. 2-When I was at university, I wore glasses. 3-When I lived in London, I went jogging every day. 4-When I worked as a gardener, I was really fit. 5-When I worked as a waiter, I got really fat. 6. When I was on holiday in France, I got flu.

LEKTION 20

1. 1-e 2-f 3-g 4-a 5-c 6-h 7-b 8-d

2. 1-True 2-False 3-True 4-True 5-False 6-True

3. 1-since 2-since 3-for 4-since 5-for 6-for 7-since 8-for

4. 1-eaten Japanese food? 2-been to a pop festival? 3-ridden a horse? 4-played golf? 5-lived in a flat? 6-drunk Australian wine? 7-broken your leg? 8-worked in a department store?

5. read, heard, seen, left, complained, taken, moved, drunk, forgotten, sung, eaten, gone, stopped, received, met, written, done

6. 1-have been 2-Did you go 3-lived 4-have you been 5-met 6-hasn't cleaned 7-have forgotten 8-left

7. received, lived, heard, finish, sleep, complained, written, like

8. 1-Have you cleaned the car yet? Yes, I've already cleaned it. 2-Have you done the shopping yet? Yes, I've already done it. 3-Have you cut the grass yet? No, I haven't cut it yet. 4-Have you washed the dishes yet? No, I haven't washed them yet. 5-Have you made the sandwiches yet? Yes, I've already made them. 6-Have you posted the letters yet? No, I haven't posted them yet.

LEKTION 21

1. 1-c 2-i 3-e 4-b 5-h 6-a 7-d 8-g 9-f

2. seen, see, heard, working, like, travelling, doing, working, saw, walking, saw, doing, talking, ask, sitting, holding, looked, talking

3. 1-find 2-ask 3-sell 4-leave 5-learn/study 6-give 7-remember 8-go to bed/sleep

4. 1-newspaper 2-hear 3-horse 4-argument 5-bring

5. 1-Really? How long have you been studying it 2-Really? How long has she been living there? 3-Really? How long has he been teaching it? 4-Really? How long has he been buying and selling them? 5-Really? How long have they been playing it? 6-Really? How long have you been working there?

6. 1-I found it when I was cleaning the cupboard. 2-I broke it when I was skiing in Austria. 3-They got married when they were living in France. 4-She called when I was talking to a

customer. 5-He lost it when he was visiting his parents.
6-I had it when I was driving to Manchester.

7. 7-3-6-9-8-2-4-1-5

8. 1-He was reading a newspaper. 2-He was eating a hamburger. 3-Yes, he was. 4-He was sitting on a sofa. 5-They were playing under the table. 6-She was crying. 7-He was holding a spoon. 8-It was standing on the table. 9-It was eating the fish.

LEKTION 22

1. hate-dislike okay-all right fat-overweight go away-leave probably-maybe press-push start-begin speak-talk look at-see

2. 1-Where does Philip want to go? 2-Will they take the children? 3-Do the children like hiking? 4-How old are the children? 5-What will the children eat? 6-Will they have a party?

3. 1-turn, handle 2-press, switch 3-pull, lever 4-turn, key 5-press, button

4. 1-tired 2-fat 3-thirsty 4-hungry 5-wet 6-cold

5. 1-himself 2-yourself 3-themselves 4-ourselves 5-myself 6-herself 7-yourselves

6. 1-unless 2-if 3-if 4-unless 5-if 6-if 7-unless 8-if

7. Einladung 1: 1, 4, 6, 7, 9, 12, 13 Einladung 2: 2, 3, 5, 8, 10, 11, 14

8. 1-They'll probably get drunk. 2-They'll probably eat hamburgers for breakfast. 3-They probably won't tidy their rooms. 4-They probably won't take the dog for a walk. 5-They'll probably sleep until 12.00. 6-They'll probably watch television all day.

LEKTION 23

1. 1-g 2-h 3-e 4-a 5-b 6-d 7-c 8-f

2. 1-He said he was leaving Bristol and going to London. 2-I asked him why he was leaving. 3-He said there were too many problems for him here. 4-I asked him what kind of problems he had. 5-He said he had all kinds of problems. 6-He said he didn't like his job, his boss didn't like him, and he was having too many problems with his girlfriends. 7-I asked him what he was going to do in London. 8-He said he didn't know yet. 9-He asked me what I was doing on Friday night. 10-I said I wasn't doing anything. 11-I asked him why. 12-He said he had two tickets to the theatre.

3. 1-d 2-g 3-e 4-f 5-c 6-a 7-b

4. 1-badly 2-really 3-usually 4-hungrily 5-quickly 6-quietly 7-angrily 8-well 9-slowly

5. 1-jealous 2-well 3-quietly 4-unhappy 5-quickly 6-hungrily 7-angry 8-loud

6. 1-He asked her if it was cold outside. 2-She asked him if he liked movies. 3-Philip asked his friend if she/he wanted another beer. 4-Dave asked Jane if she was going abroad again soon. 5-He asked her if her parents were well. 6-Jane asked Anne if her boyfriend played the guitar.

7. 1-What are you doing this weekend? 2-I'm going to a party. 3-Where's the party? 4-It's in Greenwood. It's going to be a very good party. 5-Why is it going to be a good party? 6-Because my friend's parents are going to be away for the weekend. 7-What's your friend's name? 8-My friend's name is Linda, and her brother's name is James.

8. 1-You say, 'Excuse me, can you tell me the way to the station?' 2-You say, 'Goodnight.' 3-You say, 'Excuse me, do you mind if I sit here?/next to you?' 4-You say, 'Excuse me, what time does the library close?' 5-You say, 'Would you like to see a film tonight?'

LEKTION 24

1. 1-a lot 2-dirty 3-leave 4-early 5-different 6-never 7-quiet 8-well 9-sell 10-lose

2. 1-earrings 2-borrow 3-carrot 4-horrible 5-hurry 6-married 7-sorry 8-tomorrow 9-coffee 10-different 11-difficult 12-foggy 13-skiing

3. 1-do 2-does 3-has 4-is 5-are 6-have 7-do 8-has

4. chair-wear-care, blue-do-knew-true, bread-said-red-head, steak-wake-break-make, wait-straight-late-great-weight, fight-white-height-right-night

5. 1-taller=tallest 2-snowing=snow 3-go=going 4-because=so 5-on=in 6-isn't=hasn't 7-something=anything 8-since=for

6. ACROSS: 1-musical 4-laugh 6-gone 7-stay 10-on 11-to be 13-met 14-both 17-anything 18-cut 19-because 23-pub 25-early 26-August 27-snow 28-looked badly
DOWN: 1-miss 2-ago 3-lonely 4-let's 5-hurts 8-about 9-yet 15-have 16-these 20-could 21-earn 22-slowly 23-pulls 24-bacon

7. 1-Has she called her mother yet? No, she hasn't. 2-Has she cleaned the bathroom yet? Yes, she has. 3-Has she tidied the bedrooms? Yes, she has. 4-Has she posted the letters? No, she hasn't. 5-Has she been to the library yet? Yes, she has. 6-Has she taken the dog out yet? Yes, she has.

8. 1-a 2-c 3-a 4-b. 5-a 6-c

9. It's Tuesday. It has been very hot every day, but it's raining today. The hotel is great - it's very small and quiet, but it has a big swimming pool, and two restaurants. There are lots of interesting people. We've been swimming every day. Shopping is difficult, because we don't speak the language! But the local people are very nice, and the food is wonderful. We'll be home/We're coming home on Saturday, so we'll see you then.

10. Mögliche Antworten: 1-I'm wearing (jeans.) 2-I look like my (father). 3-It's (raining) 4-I went to (Spain). 5-I go to the dentist (twice a year). 6-Yes, I have/No, I haven't. 7-I lived in (Paris). 8-I've been studying English (for three years).

Grammatik auf einen Blick

REGELMÄSSIGE VERBEN in diesem Übungsbuch

INFINITIV	PRÄTERITUM/PARTIZIP PERFEKT	INFINITIV	PRÄTERITUM/PARTIZIP PERFEKT
answer	answered	miss	missed
apologize	apologized	move	moved
arrive	arrived	need	needed
ask	asked	open	opened
believe	believed	order	ordered
borrow	borrowed	owe	owed
call	called	paint	painted
carry	carried	pass	passed
cause	caused	phone	phoned
check	checked	play	played
clean	cleaned	post	posted
close	closed	press	pressed
complain	complained	pull	pulled
cook	cooked	receive	received
crash	crashed	remember	remembered
cry	cried	reserve	reserved
dance	danced	return	returned
die	died	shout	shouted
dislike	disliked	start	started
earn	earned	stay	stayed
enjoy	enjoyed	stop	stopped
finish	finished	study	studied
happen	happened	talk	talked
hate	hated	tidy	tidied
help	helped	travel	traveled
hurry	hurried	turn	turned
include	included	type	typed
invite	invited	use	used
join	joined	visit	visited
laugh	laughed	want	wanted
live	lived	watch	watched
look	looked	whisper	whispered
marry	married	work	worked
mind	minded	worry	worried

UNREGELMÄSSIGE VERBEN in diesem Übungsbuch

INFINITIV	PRÄTERITUM	PARTIZIP PERFEKT	INFINITIV	PRÄTERITUM	PARTIZIP PERFEKT
be	was/were	been	learn	learnt/learned	learnt/learned
become	became	become	leave	left	left
begin	began	begun	lose	lost	lost
break	broke	broken	make	made	made
bring	brought	brought	meet	met	met
buy	bought	bought	pay	paid	paid
can	could	been able	read	read	read
come	came	come	ride	rode	ridden
cut	cut	cut	say	said	said
do	did	done	see	saw	seen
drink	drank	drunk	sell	sold	sold
eat	ate	eaten	shine	shone	shone
fall	fell	fallen	sing	sang	sung
feel	felt	felt	sit	sat	sat
find	found	found	sleep	slept	slept
forget	forgot	forgotten	speak	spoke	spoken
get	got	got	swim	swam	swum
give	gave	given	take	took	taken
go	went	gone/been	teach	taught	taught
have	had	had	tell	told	told
hear	heard	heard	think	thought	thought
hit	hit	hit	understand	understood	understood
hold	held	held	wear	wore	worn
hurt	hurt	hurt	write	wrote	written
know	knew	known			

Beispiele für den Gebrauch der verschiedenen Zeiten:

Präsens:

you play	you don't play	do you play?
he plays	he doesn't play	does he play?

Präteritum:

you played	you didn't play	did you play?
he played	he didn't play	did he play?

Verlaufsform Präsens:

you are (you're) playing	you aren't playing	are you playing?
he is (he's) playing	he isn't playing	is he playing?

Verlaufsform Präteritum:

you were playing	you weren't playing	were you playing?
he was playing	he wasn't playing	was he playing?

Perfekt:

| you have (you've) played | you haven't played | have you played? |
| he has (he's) played | he hasn't played | has he played? |

Verlaufsform Perfekt:

| you have (you've) been playing | you haven't been playing | have you been playing? |
| he has (he's) been playing | he hasn't been playing | has he been playing? |

KOMPARATIVE UND SUPERLATIVE

ADJEKTIV	KOMPARATIV	SUPERLATIV
cheap	cheaper	cheapest
old	older	oldest
fast	faster	fastest
tall	taller	tallest
angry	angrier	angriest
busy	busier	busiest
dirty	dirtier	dirtiest
easy	easier	easiest
hot	hotter	hottest
big	bigger	biggest
expensive	more expensive	most expensive
handsome	more handsome	most handsome
interesting	more interesting	most interesting
beautiful	more beautiful	most beautiful
good	better	best
bad	worse	worst

Beispiele:
> Jane is taller than her brother.
> I think Liz is much more beautiful than Jane.
> This is the biggest room in the house.
> I bought the most expensive shoes in the shop.

PERSONALPRONOMEN

SUBJEKTFORM	OBJEKTFORM	ADJEKTIVISCHE FORM
I	me	my
you	you	your
she	her	her
he	him	his
it	it	its
we	us	our
you	you	you
they	them	their

Beispiele:
> I don't like her very much. She always shouts at me.
> They invited us to their party.
> We told him about our holiday.

ZAHLEN

1 one	11 eleven	21 twenty-one	40 forty
2 two	12 twelve	22 twenty-two	50 fifty
3 three	13 thirteen	23 twenty-three	60 sixty
4 four	14 fourteen	24 twenty-four	70 seventy
5 five	15 fifteen	25 twenty-five	80 eighty
6 six	16 sixteen	26 twenty-six	90 ninety
7 seven	17 seventeen	27 twenty-seven	100 a hundred
8 eight	18 eighteen	28 twenty-eight	1,000 a thousand
9 nine	19 nineteen	29 twenty-nine	1,000,000 a million
10 ten	20 twenty	30 thirty	

Wie man Zahlen angibt:

397	three hundred and ninety-seven
4,850	four thousand, eight hundred and fifty
50,000	fifty thousand
650,000	six hundred and fifty thousand
1,400,000	one million, four hundred thousand

PREISE

Wie man Preise angibt:

50p	fifty pence
75p	seventy-five pence
£1.00	one pound
£1.20	one pound twenty
£8.50	eight pounds fifty
£250.00	two hundred and fifty pounds

MONATE

January	April	July	October
February	May	August	November
March	June	September	December

WOCHENTAGE

Monday	Friday
Tuesday	Saturday
Wednesday	Sunday
Thursday	

DATEN

1st first	11th eleventh	21st twenty-first
2nd second	12th twelfth	22nd twenty-second
3rd third	13th thirteenth	23rd twenty-third
4th fourth	14th fourteenth	24th twenty-fourth
5th fifth	15th fifteenth	25th twenty-fifth
6th sixth	16th sixteenth	26th twenty-sixth
7th seventh	17th seventeenth	27th twenty-seventh
8th eighth	18th eighteenth	28th twenty-eighth
9th ninth	19th nineteenth	29th twenty-ninth
10th tenth	20th twentieth	30th thirtieth
		31st thirty-first

Wie man Daten angibt:
- 3 January 1994 — The third of January, nineteen ninety-four
- 9 August 1949 — The ninth of August, nineteen forty-nine
- 5/1/91 — The fifth of January, nineteen ninety-one

UHRZEIT

Wie man die Uhrzeit angibt:
- 10:00 ten o'clock
- 11:30 half past eleven, or eleven thirty
- 2:15 quarter past two, or two fifteen
- 3:45 quarter to four, or three forty-five
- 4:10 ten past four, or four ten
- 5:40 twenty to six, or five forty
- 7:00 a.m. seven o'clock in the morning
- 3:00 p.m. three o'clock in the afternoon
- 8:00 p.m. eight o'clock in the evening

ABKÜRZUNGEN

a.m.	before noon (ante meridiem)	gm	gramme	ft	foot
p.m.	after noon (post meridiem)	lb	pound	in	inch
		oz	ounce	US	the United States
£	pound	cm	centimetre	USA	the United States of America
p	pence	m	metre	UK	United Kingdom
kg	kilogramme	km	kilometre	GB	Great Britain

GLOSSAR

Nach jedem Eintrag im Glossar finden Sie die Nummer der Lektion, in der die Vokabel zum erstenmal vorkommt.

A

a little	ein wenig, etwas 11
a lot of	viel 9
a/an	ein 2
about	um … her; über; ungefähr 6
abroad	im Ausland 16
accident	Unfall 21
accountant	Buchhalter 2
actor	Schauspieler 11
address	Adresse 1
Africa	Afrika 9
after	nach, hinter 6
afternoon	Nachmittag 15
age	Alter 1
ago	vor 20
airport	Flughafen 18
all	alle 6
all right	in Ordnung, okay 22
alone	allein 22
along	entlang; weiter-, vorwärts- 7
already	schon, bereits 20
also	auch; außerdem, ferner 9
always	immer 5
American	Amerikaner(in); amerikanisch 1
and	und 1
angrily	wütend 23
angry	zornig, verärgert 8
ankle	Knöchel 19
another	noch eine/r/s; andere/r/s 8
answer (v)	antworten 21
any	irgendein/e; jede/r/s 3
anybody	(irgend)jemand; jede/r; wer 17
anything	(irgend) etwas; alles 8
anywhere	irgendwo; überall 17
apologise (v)	sich entschuldigen 22
apple	Apfel 3
April	April 15
argument	Auseinandersetzung 8
arm	Arm 21
arrive (v)	ankommen 18
art gallery	Kunstgalerie 7
artist	Künstler 11
as	als, während; da; wie 11
ask (v)	fragen 8
aspirin	Aspirin 19
at	an, bei, in; um 4
at the end	am Schluß, am Ende 7
at the moment	im Augenblick, momentan 14
attractive	attraktiv, anziehend 9
August	August 15
aunt	Tante 2
Australia	Australien 1
Australian	Australier(in); australisch 1
away	(weit) weg 22
awful	schrecklich, furchtbar 19

B

back	zurück 18
bacon	Schinkenspeck 4
bad	schlecht, übel 2
badly	schlecht, schwer 23
badminton	Federball 4
bag	Tasche 6
ballet	Ballett 15
banana	Banane 10
bank	Bank 7
barbecue	Grillfest, Barbecue 15
bath	Bad 3
bathroom	Badezimmer 3
be (v)	sein 1
be careful	vorsichtig sein, aufpassen 17
beans	Bohnen 10
beautiful	schön 13
because	wegen, weil 11
become (v)	werden 17
bed	Bett 4
bedroom	Schlafzimmer 3
beef	Rindfleisch 10
beer	Bier 4
begin (v)	anfangen, beginnen 22
beginning	Anfang, Beginn 17
behind	hinter 3
believe (v)	glauben 9
between	zwischen 3
bicycle	Fahrrad 9
big	groß 2
birthday	Geburtstag 14
bit	Stück, Stückchen, Teil 8
black	schwarz 3
blouse	Bluse 6
blue	blau 3
body	Körper 19
book (v)	buchen, reservieren 18
book	Buch 3
boots	Stiefel 9

bored	gelangweilt 19	**class**	Klasse 16
born	geboren 9	**clean (v)**	säubern, reinigen 9
borrow (v)	sich (aus)leihen, borgen 7	**clock**	Uhr 16
boss	Chef, Boß 2	**close (v)**	schließen 7
both	beide 14	**closed**	geschlossen 7
boyfriend	Freund 5	**clothes**	Kleider 14
branch	Zweig; Filiale, Zweigstelle 2	**centimetre (cm.)**	Zentimeter 13
Brazil	Brasilien 1	**coach**	Kutsche; Waggon, Trainer 9
Brazilian	Brasilianer(in); brasilianisch 1	**coat**	Mantel 6
bread	Brot 10	**coffee**	Kaffee 1
break (v)	(zer)brechen 17	**cold (n)**	Kälte 20
breakfast	Frühstück 4	**cold**	kalt 9
bridge	Brücke 7	**colleague**	Kollege 17
bring (v)	bringen 15	**colour**	Farbe 6
brochure	Broschüre 9	**come (v)**	kommen 5
brother	Bruder 2	**come on (v)**	nachkommen 22
brown	braun 3	**company**	Gesellschaft; Firma 2
buffet	Buffet 18	**complain (v)**	sich beklagen, klagen über 20
building	Gebäude 3	**complaint**	Beschwerde 20
bus	Bus 9	**computer**	Computer 3
busy	beschäftigt 5	**concert**	Konzert 15
but	aber 3	**cook (n)**	Koch 19
butcher	Metzger 7	**cook (v)**	kochen 5
button	Knopf 22	**cooking (n)**	Kochen, Essen; Küche 6
buy (v)	kaufen 6	**corner**	Ecke 3
by	an, neben; bis 9	**cotton**	Baumwolle 6
by the way	übrigens 7	**Could I/you ...?**	könnte ich/könntest du ...? 18
		crash (v)	verunglücken, einen Unfall haben 17

C

cake	Kuchen 19	**credit card**	Kreditkarte 18
calendar	Kalender 16	**crossroads**	Kreuzung 7
call (v)	(an)rufen 8	**cry (v)**	weinen; rufen, schreien 21
camera	Kamera; Fotoapparat 15	**cup**	Tasse 10
camp site	Camping-, Zeltplatz 9	**cupboard**	Schrank 21
camping	Camping, Zelten 9	**customer**	Kunde 21
Can I help you?	kann ich Ihnen helfen? 6	**cut (v)**	schneiden 20
can (v)	können 11		

D

Canada	Kanada 1	**dad**	Vati 4
Canadian	Kanadier(in); kanadisch 1	**dance (v)**	tanzen 9
car	Auto, Wagen 2	**dancing**	Tanzen 4
carpet	Teppich 3	**dark**	dunkel 13
carrots	Karotten 10	**date (appointment)**	Termin 8
carry (v)	tragen 14	**date (day/month)**	Datum 15
casual	Freizeit- 6	**daughter**	Tochter 2
cat	Katze 3	**day**	Tag 14
cause (v)	verursachen 17	**day-return**	Tagesrückfahrkarte 18
chair	Stuhl 3	**December**	Dezember 15
change (v)	verändern 16	**dentist**	Zahnarzt 11
cheap	billig 6	**department**	Abteilung 7
check (v)	überprüfen; nachsehen 9	**desk**	Schreibtisch 3
cheese	Käse 10	**dessert**	Dessert, Nachspeise 19
chef	Küchenchef; Koch 11	**diary**	Tagebuch 15
chicken	Hähnchen 10	**die (v)**	sterben 23
child (children)	Kind (Kinder) 2	**diet**	Diät 17
chin	Kinn 13	**different**	andere/r/s; verschieden, unterschiedlich 16
chips	Pommes frites 10		
church	Kirche 7	**difficult**	schwierig 5
cinema	Kino 15		

dinner	Abendessen 5	**feel (v)**	fühlen, spüren 19
dirty	schmutzig 18	**festival**	Fest; Festival, Festspiele 20
disco	Disko 9	**fifth**	fünfte/r 7
dislike (v)	nicht mögen 22	**fight**	Kampf 21
do (v)	tun, machen 5	**film**	Film 15
do you ever ...?	machst du je …? 16	**find (v)**	finden 21
do you mind if ...?	macht es dir etwas aus, wenn … 16	**fine**	schön, fein 15
dog	Hund 15	**finish (v)**	beenden 5
don't worry	keine Sorge 11	**first**	erste/r/s; zuerst, als erstes 7
door	Tür 3	**first name**	Vorname 2
down	herunter, hinunter; unten 22	**fish**	Fisch 6
dress	Kleid 14	**fit**	fit, gesund 19
drink (v)	trinken 5	**five**	fünf 1
driver	Fahrer 11	**flat**	Wohnung 14
drunk	betrunken (Adjektiv)13	**flight**	Flug 18
drunkenly	betrunken (Adverb) 23	**floor**	Boden; Stock(werk) 7
		flu	Grippe 19

E

		fog	Nebel 14
		foggy	neblig 14
early	früh 19	**food**	Essen, Nahrung; Lebensmittel 5
earn (v)	verdienen 21	**foot**	Fuß 19
earrings	Ohrringe 13	**football**	Fußball 5
ears	Ohren 13	**for**	für 6; seit, während 20
easy	einfach, leicht 6	**for ages**	eine Ewigkeit, ewig lang 21
eat (v)	essen 5	**foreign**	ausländisch 11
eat out (v)	zum Essen ausgehen 9	**forget (v)**	vergessen 20
economics	Volkswirtschaft, Wirtschaftswissenschaften 9	**four**	vier 1
egg	Ei 3	**fourth**	vierte/r 7
eight	acht 1	**France**	Frankreich 1
eighth	achte/r 7	**free**	frei 5
elbow	Ellbogen 19	**free time**	Freizeit 16
end	Ende 17	**French**	französisch 1
engine	Maschine; Motor 22	**Friday**	Freitag 5
engineer	Ingenieur 2	**fridge**	Kühlschrank 3
England	England 1	**friend**	Freund, Bekannter 5
English	Engländer(in); englisch 1	**from**	von; aus 1
enjoy (v)	genießen; sich amüsieren 9	**fruit**	Obst 10
Europe	Europa 9	**fun**	Spaß 9
evening	Abend 5	**funny**	witzig, komisch 23
ever	je(mals) 20	**future**	Zukunft 17
every	jede/r/s 9		

G

exam	Examen, Prüfung 17	**gallon (gal.)**	Gallone 10
excuse me	Entschuldigung 2	**game**	Spiel 16
exercise	Übung 10	**garage**	Garage 3
expensive	teuer 6	**garden**	Garten 3
extra	zusätzlich; extra, besonders 19	**gardener**	Gärtner 19
		German	Deutsche(r); deutsch 1

F

		Germany	Deutschland 1
fair	gerecht, fair; blond, hell 13	**get (v)**	bekommen, erhalten 17
fall (v)	fallen 17	**get married (v)**	heiraten 9
false	falsch 13	**get up (v)**	aufstehen 5
family	Familie 5	**girlfriend**	Freundin 1
far	weit 7	**give (v)**	geben 15
fast	schnell 23	**glass**	Glas 10
fat	dick, fett 1	**glasses**	Brille 13
father	Vater 2	**gloves**	Handschuhe 6
February	Februar 15	**go (v)**	gehen 5

go ahead (v)	vorangehen, vorausgehen 16	here	hier 4
go camping (v)	zelten gehen 9	here it is	hier ist es 6
go for a walk (v)	spazierengehen 15	herself	sie selbst 22
go shopping (v)	einkaufen 8	hey!	he! 7
go skiing (v)	zum Skilaufen fahren 9	hi	hallo 2
go to bed (v)	zu, ins Bett gehen 5	high	hoch 13
golf	Golf 15	hiking	Wandern 9
good	gut 2	him	ihn; ihm 4
good idea	gute Idee 6	himself	er selbst 22
good luck	viel Glück 19	his	sein; seine/r/s 1
good morning	guten Morgen 1	hit (v)	schlagen, hauen; treffen 21
goodbye	Auf Wiedersehen 2	Hold on a minute.	Moment mal 15
grandchild	Enkel(kind) 2	hold (v)	halten 21
grandfather	Großvater 2	holiday	Urlaub, Ferien 9
grandmother	Großmutter 2	home	Heim, Zuhause; Heimat 5
grass	Gras 20	horrible	schrecklich 10
great	groß; großartig 14	horse	Pferd 9
great time	tolle Zeit 9	hospital	Krankenhaus 21
green	grün 3	hot	warm, heiß 9
guide	Führer 11	hotel	Hotel 3
guitar	Gitarre 5	hour	Stunde 18
gym	Turnhalle; Fitneßcenter 3	house	Haus 3
		How about ...ing?	wie wäre es mit...? 15
		How nice to see you.	wie schön, dich/Sie/euch zu sehen 21

H

hair	Haar 13	How about...?	wie wäre es mit …? 5
half past (time)	halb (zwei usw.) 4	How are you?	wie geht's? 2
ham	Schinken 10	How do you do?	guten Tag/Abend; (formell) angenehm 1
hamburger	Hamburger (Frikadelle) 10	how long?	wie lange? 21
hand	Hand 19	how many?	wie viele? 3
handle	Griff 22	how much?	wieviel? 6
handsome	hübsch 13	how old?	wie alt? 2
hangover	Kater 19	hungrily	hungrig 23
happen (v)	geschehen, sich ereignen 8	hungry	hungrig 10
happily	glücklich; glücklicherweise 23	hurry (v)	sich beeilen 22
happy	glücklich; heiter 13	hurt (v)	verletzen, sich weh tun; kränken 19
hard	hart 22	husband	Ehemann 2
has/have got	hat/habe(n) bekommen 2		
hat	Hut 14		
hate (v)	hassen 4		
have (v)	haben 5		

I

have a drink (v)	etwas trinken (gehen) 7	I don't believe you.	ich glaube dir nicht 9
have a shower/bath (v)	duschen/baden 5	I don't care.	Das ist mir egal. 20
have lunch (v)	zu Mittag essen 5	I see.	Aha!/Verstehe! 2
have you ever ...?	hast du/haben Sie/habt ihr je …? 20	I think so.	ich glaube schon 15
he	er 1	I'd like...	ich möchte, hätte gern... 10
head	Kopf 19	I'd/we'd love to.	das würde ich/würden wir sehr gern (tun)/mit Vergnügen 15
headache	Kopfschmerzen 19	I'm fine	mir geht's gut 2
health	Gesundheit 17	I'm sorry	Entschuldigung, tut mir leid 1
healthy	gesund 17	if	wenn; falls 22
hear (from) (v)	hören (von) 17	ill	krank 19
hear (v)	hören 20	important	wichtig 11
hear about (v)	von etw. hören 21	in	in; mit 3
heavy	schwer 13	in fact	in der Tat, tatsächlich; eigentlich 4
height	Höhe; Größe 13	in front of	vor 15
hello	hallo 2	include (v)	einschließen, enthalten 18
help (v)	helfen 19	India	Indien 9
her	ihr 1		

India	Indien 1	**letter**	Brief 5
Indian	Inder(in) 1	**lettuce**	Kopfsalat 10
inside	innen, drinn(en) 7	**lever**	Hebel 22
interesting	interessant 5	**library**	Bücherei, Bibliothek 7
international	international 2	**life**	Leben 5
into	in; gegen 7	**light (n)**	Licht 22
invitations	Einladungen 17	**light**	leicht 13
invite (v)	einladen 15	**like**	ähnlich; wie 4
Ireland	Irland 9	**listen to (v)**	zuhören 16
it	es 1	**litre**	Liter 10
it doesn't matter	es ist egal, macht nichts 17	**live (v)**	leben 5
Italy	Italien 1	**living room**	Wohnzimmer 3
Italian	Italiener(in) 1	**lobby**	Hotelhalle 3
		lonely	einsam 19
		long	lang 13

J

jacket	Jacke 6	**look (appearance) (v)**	aussehen, scheinen 19
January	Januar 15	**look (v)**	gucken, schauen; sehen 8
Japan	Japan 1	**look at (v)**	ansehen, anschauen 16
Japanese	Japaner(in); japanisch 1	**look forward to (v)**	sich freuen auf 15
jazz	Jazz 20	**look like (v)**	ausehen wie 13
jealous	eifersüchtig 17	**lose (v)**	verlieren 19
jealously	Eifersucht 23	**lots of**	viel/e 11
jeans	Jeans 6	**loud**	laut 23
jet-lagged	an Jet-lag leidend 19	**love**	Liebe 4
job	Arbeit, Job 2	**lunch**	Mittagessen 10
jogging	Jogging 8	**lunchtime**	Mittagszeit 20
join (v)	verbinden; sich anschließen 19		
July	Juli 15		
June	Juni 15		
just	gerade, (so)eben 8		
just a minute	einen Moment mal 16		

M

		magazine	Zeitschrift, Magazin 14
		make (v)	machen 11
		manager	Geschäftsführer, Manager 18
		many	viele 20
		March	März 15
		married	verheiratet 1
		marry (v)	heiraten 22
		May	Mai 15
		maybe	vielleicht 6
		me	mich; mir 4
		meat	Fleisch 4
		medium	mittlere/r/s 6
		meet (v)	treffen, kennenlernen 5
		meeting	Treffen 15
		men	Männer 7
		milk	Milch 10
		mind (v)	sich kümmern, sich etw. daraus machen 16

K

key	Schlüssel 22	**minute**	Minute 16
kilogram (kg)	Kilogramm (kg) 10	**miss (v)**	verpassen; vermissen 22
kitchen	Küche 3	**mistake**	Fehler 2
knee	Knie 19	**Monday**	Montag 5
knife	Messer 3	**money**	Geld 7
know (v)	kennen; wissen 6	**month**	Monat 16
		more	mehr 10
		morning	Morgen 4
		mother	Mutter 2
		motorbike	Motorrad 9
		mountain	Berg 13
		mouth	Mund 13

L

label	Schild, Etikett 6
lamb	Lamm 10
language	Sprache 11
large	groß 6
last night	gestern abend/nacht 11
last week	letzte Woche 10
last year	letztes Jahr 9
late	spät 4
laugh (v)	lachen 21
learn (v)	lernen; erfahren 5
leather	Leder 13
leave (v)	verlassen, weggehen 18
left	links 3
leg	Bein 19
lemon	Zitrone 10
lesson	Lektion 16
let's see	mal sehen 16

move (v)	bewegen 9	only	nur 8
Mr	Herr 1	open (v)	öffnen, aufmachen 10
Ms	Fräulein 1	open	offen 7
mum	Mama 4	opera	Oper 11
museum	Museum 15	opposite	gegenüber; entgegengesetzt 7
music	Musik 20	or	oder 3
musical instrument	Musikinstrument 16	orange	orange(farben) 3
my	mein 1	order (v)	bestellen 10
myself	ich selbst; mich, mir 22	ounce (oz.)	Unze 10
		our	unser 4
		ourselves	uns; wir selbst 22
		outside	außen; draußen 7
		over	über 7
		over there	dort drüben 16
		overweight	zu schwer, übergewichtig 19
		owe (v)	schulden 18

N

name	Name 1
nationality	Nationalität 1
near	nahe, in der Nähe 3
nearly	fast 20
neck	Hals 13
need (v)	brauchen, benötigen 17
neither	auch nicht; weder...noch 21
nephew	Neffe 2
Never mind	macht nichts 15
never	nie(mals) 5
new	neu 2
news	Nachrichten, Neuigkeiten 2
newspaper	Zeitung 5
next to	neben 3
next year	nächstes Jahr 10
nice	nett; sympathisch 2
niece	Nichte 2
night	Nacht 8
nine	neun 1
ninth	neunte/r 7
no	nein 1
no, thank you	nein danke 4
noise	Lärm 20
nose	Nase 13
not... any more	nicht...mehr 19
not... at all	überhaupt...nicht 4
nothing	nichts 16
November	November 15
now	nun, jetzt 2
nurse	Krankenschwester 11

O

o'clock	(fünf) Uhr 4
October	Oktober 15
of course	natürlich 16
office	Büro 2
often	oft, häufig 5
oh dear	o je 21
oil	Öl 9
okay	okay, in Ordnung 2
old	alt 13
omelette	Omelett 10
on	auf; an 3
on the phone	am Telefon 15
one (n)	Eins 6
one	ein/eine/ein; eine/r/s 1
onion	Zwiebel 10

P

pain	Schmerz/en 19
paint (v)	malen 11
painter	Maler 11
parents	Eltern 5
park	Park 3
part-time	Teilzeit- 16
partner	Partner 17
party	Party 11
pass an exam (v)	eine Prüfung bestehen 17
patient	Patient 21
pay (v)	(be)zahlen 18
pear	Birne 10
peas	Erbsen 10
pen	Füllfederhalter; Kugelschreiber 18
pence	Pence 6
people	Menschen, Leute 3
person	Person 8
phone (v)	telefonieren 14
photograph	Foto 13
photographer	Fotograf 2
photography	Fotografie 16
pianist	Klavierspieler, Pianist 11
piano	Klavier 11
pilot	Pilot 11
pink	rosa 3
pint (pt)	Pint (Maß) 10
pizza	Pizza 10
plane	Flugzeug; Ebene 9
platform	Bahnsteig; Plattform 18
play (v)	spielen 5
play	Spiel; Stück (Theater) 16
please	bitte 1
pleased to meet you	freut mich, Sie kennenzulernen 1
poetry	Dichtkunst, Poesie 5
police	Polizei 20
policeman	Polizist 2
pop	Popmusik 20
popular	beliebt 6

pork	Schweinefleisch 10	**sandwich**	Sandwich, belegtes Brot 3
post (v)	(Brief) aufgeben, einwerfen 17	**Saturday**	Samstag 5
post office	Post[amt] 7	**sauna**	Sauna 3
postcard	Postkarte 14	**sausage**	Wurst, Würstchen 4
postman	Postbote 11	**say (v)**	sagen 23
potato	Kartoffel 10	**scarf**	Hals-, Kopftuch 14
pound (£)	Pfund (Währungseinheit) 6	**Scotland**	Schottland 1
pound (lb.)	Pfund (Gewicht) 10	**Scottish**	schottisch 1
present	anwesend, gegenwärtig 6	**sea**	Meer, See 9
press (v)	drücken 22	**second**	zweite/r 7
pretty	hübsch 8	**secretary**	Sekretär/in 11
price	Preis 6	**see (v)**	sehen 8
probably	wahrscheinlich 20	**sell (v)**	verkaufen 21
problem	Problem 8	**sensible**	vernünftig 22
pub	Pub 4	**September**	September 15
public	Öffentlichkeit 3	**seven**	sieben 1
pull (v)	ziehen 22	**seventh**	siebte/r 7
purple	purpur, violett 3	**she**	sie 1

Q

		shine (v)	leuchten, glänzen; polieren 14
quarter	Viertel 5	**shirt**	Hemd 6
quarter past	viertel nach 5	**shoes**	Schuhe 6
quarter to	viertel vor 5	**shop**	Laden, Geschäft 3
questions	Fragen 11	**shopping**	Einkaufen; Einkäufe 4
quickly	schnell 18	**short**	kurz 13
quiet	ruhig 14	**shout (v)**	rufen, schreien 23
quietly	leise, ruhig 23	**shower**	Dusche 3
quite	ganz 4	**sick**	krank, übel 19

R

		sightseeing	Besichtigungen, Sightseeing 9
radio	Radio 16	**sign**	Zeichen 7
rain	Regen 14	**silk**	Seide 6
rather	ziemlich 13	**sing (v)**	singen 11
read (v)	lesen 5	**singer**	Sänger/in 11
ready	fertig, bereit 4	**single**	einzige/r/s; einzeln; ledig 1
really	wirklich, tatsächlich 8	**sink**	Waschbecken 3
really?	echt? 9	**sister**	Schwester 2
receive (v)	empfangen, erhalten 20	**sit (v)**	sitzen 14
red	rot 3	**six**	sechs 1
remember (v)	sich erinnern 14	**sixth**	sechste/r 7
reporter	Reporter 2	**size**	Größe 6
restaurant	Restaurant 3	**skating**	Schlittschuhlaufen 14
return (ticket) (n)	Rückfahrkarte 18	**skiing**	Skifahren 9
return (v)	zurückkehren, -kommen 18	**skirt**	Rock 6
rich	reich 17	**sleep (n)**	Schlaf 17
ride (v)	reiten; fahren 11	**sleep (v)**	schlafen 14
right	richtig, recht; rechte/r/s 3	**sleepily**	schläfrig 23
right now	sofort 14	**slim**	schlank 13
river	Fluß 7	**slowly**	langsam 23
road	Straße 7	**small**	klein 2
room	Zimmer 17	**snow**	Schnee 14
run (v)	laufen, rennen 21	**snowing**	Schneegestöber 14

S

		so	so; da, es 14
		soap	Seife 3
		socially	gesellschaftlich, sozial 17
		socks	Socken 6
sad	traurig 13	**sofa**	Sofa 3
sadly	traurig(erweise) 23	**some**	ein paar, einige, manche/r/s 3
salad	Salat 10	**somebody**	jemand 16
same	der/die/das gleiche 5	**something**	etwas 17

sometimes	manchmal 5	teeth	Zähne 13
somewhere	irgendwo 17	telephone	Telefon 3
son	Sohn 2	telephone box	Telefonzelle, -häuschen 7
song	Lied 11	telephone call	Anruf 17
Sorry to bother you.	es tut mir leid, Sie zu belästigen 15	television	Fernsehen 3
sorry	Entschuldigung!, Verzeihung! 1	tell (v)	erzählen, sagen 8
soup	Suppe 10	ten	zehn 1
Spain	Spanien 1	tennis	Tennis 5
Spanish	spanisch 1	tent	Zelt 9
speak (v)	reden, sprechen 11	tenth	zehnte/r 7
spoon	Löffel 21	terrible	schrecklich 18
sports	Sport 3	thank you	danke 1
sports centre	Sportzentrum 18	that	das; daß 5
stamps	Briefmarken 7	that's right	das stimmt 13
start (v)	anfangen; (Motor) starten 5	the	der/die/das 3
station	Bahnhof 15	theatre	Theater 15
stay (v)	bleiben 9	their	ihr; seine/r/s 4
stay up (v)	aufbleiben 22	them	sie; ihnen 4
steak	Steak 10	themselves	sich; sie selbst 22
still	noch 4	then	dann; da; von da an 7
stomach	Magen, Bauch 19	there	dort, da; dorthin, dahin 7
stop (v)	anhalten, stoppen 20	there is/are	da ist/sind 3
story	Geschichte 8	these	diese/r/s 6
straight ahead	geradeaus 7	they	sie; man 1
straight on	gerade(aus) 7	thing	Ding, Sache 15
strange	seltsam, sonderbar 5	think (v)	denken 23
strawberry	Erdbeere 10	third	dritte/r 7
street	Straße 7	thirsty	durstig 19
strong	stark, kräftig 13	this	dies, das 4
student	Student/in 9	this/that way	hier entlang/dort entlang 7
study (v)	studieren 9	those	jene/r/s 9
suit	Anzug 14	three	drei 1
summer	Sommer 9	Thursday	Donnerstag 5
sun	Sonne 14	ticket	Fahr-, Flugkarte, Ticket, Eintrittskarte 16
Sunday	Sonntag 5	tidy (v)	aufräumen 20
supermarket	Supermarkt 6	tie	Krawatte 6
surprised	überrascht 8	time	Zeit 4
sweater	Pullover 6	tired	müde 19
swim (v)	schwimmen 7	to	zu; bis 5
swimming	Schwimmen 4	today	heute 14
swimming pool	Swimmingpool 3	toilet	Toilette 3
switch	Schalter 22	tomato	Tomate 10
		tomorrow	morgen 5

T

table	Tisch 3	tonight	heute abend, heute nacht 14
take (a size) (v)	Maß nehmen 6	too	auch 3
take (time) (v)	sich Zeit lassen 18	too much	zuviel, zu viele 19
take (v)	nehmen 15	toothache	Zahnschmerzen 19
take care (v)	aufpassen, vorsichtig sein 14	tour group	Reisegruppe 18
talk (v)	sprechen, reden 21	tour guide	Reiseführer 11
tall	groß, hoch 13	tourist	Tourist(in) 7
taxi	Taxi 9	train	Zug 9
taxi driver	Taxifahrer 18	travel (v)	reisen 9
tea	Tee 1	travel (n)	Reise 2
teach (v)	unterrichten, jmd. etw. beibringen 11	travellers' cheques	Reiseschecks 18
teacher	Lehrer 2	travelling	Reisen 9
		trip	Reise; Ausflug, Tour 19
		true	wahr, echt 13

Tuesday	Dienstag 5	well (skillfully)	gut 8
Turkey	Türkei 9	wet	naß 9
turn (v)	drehen; verwandeln 7	what kind?	was für eine Art? 17
two	zwei 1	what time?	um wieviel Uhr? 4
type (v)	tippen 11	What's on?	was wird gegeben, gezeigt, gespielt? 15
typing	Maschineschreiben, Tippen 16	what?	was?, wie? 4

U

umbrella	Regenschirm 3	when I was ...	als ich...war 19
uncle	Onkel 2	when?	wann? 8
under	unter 3	where?	wo? 1
underground	Untergrund; U-Bahn 18	which?	welche/r/s? 7
understand (v)	verstehen, begreifen 7	whisky	Whisky 16
unfit	ungeeignet, untauglich 19	whisper (v)	flüstern 23
unhappy	unglücklich 23	white	weiß 3
United States	Vereinigte Staaten 1	who?	wer? 4
university	Universität 9	Why don't you ...?	warum tust du nicht...? 19
unless	es sei denn 22	why?	warum? 8
until	bis 7	wife	Ehefrau 2
us	uns 4	will	Wille, Willen; Testament 22
use (v)	benützen, verwenden 11	wind	Wind 14
usually	gewöhnlich 5	window	Fenster 3
		windy	windig 14

V

vegetables	Gemüse 10	wine	Wein 4
vegetarian	Vegetarier(in) 4	winter	Winter 9
very	sehr 2	with	mit 7
very much	sehr 4	woman	Frau 2
vet	Tierarzt 11	wonderful	wunderbar, -voll 19
video	Video 16	word processor	Text(verarbeitungs)system, -anlage 11
visit (v)	besuchen 5	work (n)	Arbeit 5
		work (v)	arbeiten 5

W

waiter	Kellner, Ober 11	world	Welt 13
walk (n)	(Spazier)Gang 20	worry (v)	beunruhigen, Sorgen machen 22
wallet	Brieftasche 21	Would you like to ...?	würdest du gern... 15
want (v)	wünschen, mögen 6	Would you like ...?	möchtest du...? 10
want to (v)	wollen 18	wrist	Handgelenk 19
wash (v)	waschen 14	write (v)	schreiben 5
washing machine	Waschmaschine 3		

Y

watch (v)	beobachten, zusehen 5	year	Jahr 9
watch (n)	Armbanduhr; Wache 6	yellow	gelb 3
water	Wasser 9	yes	ja 1
we	wir 1	yesterday	gestern 8
wear (v)	tragen 6	yet	noch; bis jetzt, bisher 17
weather	Wetter 11	yogurt	Joghurt 10
Wednesday	Mittwoch 5	you	du/Sie 1
week	Woche 10	you can't miss it	du kannst es nicht verpassen 7
weekday	Wochentag 7	young	jung 13
weekend	Wochenende 5	your	dein/euer/Ihr 1
weight	Gewicht 13	yourself	dich; du selbst 22
Welcome back.	willkommen daheim 19	yourselves	euch; ihr selbst 22
well (not ill)	gesund 11	yuk!	igitt! 4